SEEING REALITY AS IT IS

How our Beliefs and Genetic Chaperones shape our perceptions

Joseph L. Giovannoli, BE, JD

Research Associates, LLC

Library of Congress Cataloging-in-Publication Data

Includes biographical references and index.

ISBN: 978-1-7333393-0-8 (paper)
ISBN: 978-1-7333393-1-5 EPUB (e-book)
ISBN: 978-1-7333393-2-2 Mobi (e-book)

Research Associates, LLC, Park Ridge, NJ

Website

SEEINGREALITYASITIS.COM

To Shirley Wescott,

my wife, my partner,

and my raison d'être.

Contents

Chapter 1

Chapter 2

Chapter 3

Chapter 4

Chapter 5

Chapter 6

Epilogue   115

Index

Notes to the reader

On the website **seeingrealityasitis.com** there are two essays that provide the context for a number of concepts and processes dealt within this book. The first is *Creation According to Science*, which describes our understanding of the early universe from just after the Big Bang to the formation of our sun and Earth. The second essay is *Brain Evolution*, which examines how our brains evolved from simple arrangements of neurons to become what they are today. It examines how DNA self-organized, how it enabled cells to cooperate, and how small DNA mutations made significant alterations in our appearance and abilities. The essay also describes how natural philosophers before Darwin thought evolution functioned. It also provides a description of the progression from early life on Earth through to sea creatures venturing onto land, ending with humans having brains that enabled our ancestors to create large-scale social evolution.

This book employs new concepts to explain why we see the same reality in different ways. For this reason, **bold text is used to focus attention on key ideas that combine to create a context for the reader. Reading the bold text first, therefore, is likely to make a detailed reading more productive.** Please note that devoutly religious readers might find some aspects of this book to be disconcerting.

From time to time, as examples of things described in the book occur they will be added to the seeingrealityasitis.com website.

"...there is much here that is deeply fascinating and may prove to be very persuasive...An original, highly intriguing theory on how and why beliefs are formed, inherited, and transmitted."

Kirkus Reviews

Preface

As a generalist with a science education, I began research for this book by reading scientific, historical, and other scholarly publications to identify works that might contribute towards an explanation of the different ways in which scientists and theologians perceive reality. It soon became apparent that the relation of science and religion is just one example of how our brains and cultures shape the way we each perceive reality. I would have much preferred to read a collaborative work by specialist scholars that explained the processes that make it so difficult to agree on what reality is. However, after concluding that such collaboration is unlikely in the near future, **I wrote this book to share my thoughts on how existing knowledge might be combined to explain why our views of reality are so varied.**

Discussing subjects such as the relation of science and religion can involve knowledge in fields such as genetics, neuroscience, psychology, sociology, history, genetic algorithms, biological evolution, and belief-system formation. I recall Carl Sagan discussing the problem of dealing with subjects in which he was not an authority. Given his academic position, he had his science-fiction manuscripts vetted by colleagues in other scientific disciplines. Without an array of vetting resources, writing about multidisciplinary subjects is a bit like walking a tightrope without a net. Perhaps artificial intelligence will resolve the vetting issue in the near future.

This book, written for the general reader from the perspective of a science writer,

combines research from various scientific disciplines to clarify how our brains and cultures shape the lenses through which we each perceive reality in our own way. Extensive appendices at the end of this book and on the website **seeingrealityasitis.com** are provided to give a broader context for the concepts discussed in the book. While references to scholarly works are noted at the end, my views are preceded by phrases such as "in my view", "it seems", "it appears that", and the like.

Joseph L. Giovannoli

Chapter 1

If there is only one reality, why can't we agree on what it is?

In our own way, each one of us believes we see reality as it is. We can't all be right --- or can we? This book will explore the complexity and many faces of your perceptions. You will discover the true nature of your own beliefs and the biases we all have. If you have never delved into this subject, you might just walk away with a new and powerful understanding of how to relate to our world. Imagine experiencing the world with your eyes wide open to the many influences that created your own personal reality. Imagine further being able to recognize instantly when someone is trying to influence your beliefs or lift the veil of those who might use your personal biases and beliefs to their own benefit.

Most people drift through life shaking their heads at those whose views they disagree with while they embrace their own views as true reality. When you have completed this book you will realize there is no one way to see reality. You will have started down your own personal path to understanding yourself and the beliefs of those around you. For some, it will be the first time in their lives that they encounter seeing reality as it is.

Your book creates in me an entirely different perspective on how I go about my life, what I expect from others, and what I expect from myself.

Thomas Tonon, PhD, Princeton

Our history appears to be a series of ongoing disagreements over what is real or true. Today, we disagree about climate change, biological evolution, culture wars, the damaging effects of junk science, fake news, and which sect is the true religion. Everyone involved in these disagreements thinks that their perception of reality is accurate, but with just one reality, they can't all be right. **Seeing ourselves as rational beings who make rational, objective decisions assumes that our brains provide us with true perceptions of reality. Actually, Nature provided us with brains to help us to survive, not necessarily to provide accurate perceptions of reality. Before we acquired the ability to reason, we relied on Nature to keep us alive with brain adaptations that chaperoned us through life. Those adaptations enhanced the likelihood of our ancestors' survival by guiding their thinking, their responses to stimuli, and most importantly, how they perceived reality.**

The environments in which our ancient ancestors lived threatened their existence in countless ways. Ancestors with genetic adaptations that enabled them to prevail in life-threatening encounters with predators, competitors, and the forces of Nature were able to survive. From generation to generation, successful genetic adaptations were passed to the descendants of survivors while the family lines of those without such adaptations went extinct.

While the challenges you face today are very different from those of your ancient ancestors, you deal with them using the same mental biases and traits your Stone Age ancestors used to relate to their world. **The brain you inherited alters your perceptions of reality in a way that chaperones your behaviors. Inasmuch as your adaptations operate non-consciously, you are not likely to realize when those adaptations are influencing your responses, thoughts, and perceptions.** If you engage in exchanges regarding cultural values or fake news, your Stone Age adaptations will silently influence how you perceive and respond during those exchanges. In ways such as these, your Stone Age survival adaptations influence how you perceive reality.

Dr. Donald Hoffman, a cognitive scientist, recently used what are called genetic algorithms to determine whether organisms that "see" reality as it is were more likely to survive than organisms that ignored reality in favor of their fitness to survive. The genetic algorithms he used produced useful results because biological evolution is a mathematically precise science, and genetic algorithms are the mathematical equivalent of the biological code found in our DNA. That code is a form of genetic knowledge that shapes our bodies and influences our behaviors by accumulating small beneficial changes from generation to generation. After Dr. Hoffman ran thousands of computer simulations over many generations of computer organisms, he concluded that:

> **In almost every simulation, organisms that see none of reality, but are just tuned to fitness, drive to extinction all the organisms that perceive reality as it is. So the bottom line is evolution does not favor veridical [truthful] or accurate perceptions. Those perceptions of reality go extinct.**[1]

A more detailed description of genetic algorithms can be found in Appendix C.

If the genes that influence the way we perceive reality evolved according to the same principles as Dr. Hoffman's genetic algorithms, one might realistically conclude that, **over generations of competing to survive, our ancestors' brains accumulated various genetic adaptations that improved their fitness to survive at the expense of their ability to see reality as it is. Those genetic adaptations are survival-enhancing brain traits, biases, and neurochemical influences that chaperone each of us through life.**[2] **The individual biases, brain traits, and neurochemical influences you inherited—what I refer to collectively as your "genetic chaperone"—are the subject of the next chapter.**

Chapter 2

How biases and brain traits influence our perceptions

As you read this chapter, view these individual biases and brain traits through the lens of how they provided a survival benefit to your ancestors and how today, they might or might not provide you with an advantage. One thing is certain: they can cause you to perceive reality in ways that can be fictitious or inaccurate.

Biases

The term "bias" refers to an inherited thinking preference or inclination. Such biases can be fictitious perceptions that guide our thinking by altering the way we perceive reality. Confidence-building biases, for example, influence what we believe by providing us with illusions of enhanced capabilities and expectations of success. The power of these biases underlies the wisdom of the Roman poet Virgil (70–19 BCE), who said, "They can conquer who believe they can." In addition to raising our confidence, our biases can exaggerate the importance of our goals, exaggerate how we perceive the likelihood that we will succeed, exaggerate threats, alter the way we remember facts in a way that assists us in convincing others to give us what we want, and cause us to believe we're more capable than we are. The disadvantage of not believing that we can succeed was described in a quote attributed to Henry Ford: "Whether you think you can, or you think you can't, you're right."[1] Helping us to believe we can succeed is why coaches give confidence-building talks to their sports teams.[2] This is true of business and military leaders as well.

An essential requirement of confidence-building and other illusions is that we are unaware that our biases are creating them, for illusions cannot exist once we know they are illusions. Being unaware of our biases makes possible our illusion that we have more control than we have. It is possible that perceptual illusions created by our biases cause us to see ourselves as pulling the strings that control our lives. It is more likely, however, that Nature is the puppeteer and the strings it pulls are made of perception-altering strands of DNA that form our genetic chaperones.

In their own way, each of the following biases has provided a benefit by altering how we see reality. Winning a few ball games while wearing a particular hat might result in your making the illusory correlation that wearing that hat is the reason you won. This **illusory correlation bias** inclines you to think there's a relationship between things and events where no relationship exists. In this case, you think you can control the outcome of the next game by recreating the correlation between wearing the hat and winning the game. While this illusion might give you confidence that you will win, it also underlies superstition and magical thinking.

The **optimism bias** can cause you to expect a positive outcome from a situation, even if there's no basis in reality to support your expectation. This bias might have survival or other value by replacing fear with an expectation that you will succeed.

Overestimating the control you have over events is caused by the **illusion of control** bias. It's an expectation of control that is common among gamblers and those who believe that superstitions are real. This illusion becomes stronger when you are under stress or in competition. In a similar way, the **egocentric bias** distorts your self-perception and makes you think you're more able than you really are.

The **superiority bias or illusion of superiority bias** is one that increases your self-confidence by causing you to overestimate your abilities while underestimating your deficiencies. Another bias that enhances your self-image is the **self-serving bias.** It inclines you to reject valid criticism and to stress your attributes or achievements while ignoring your shortcomings.

We have all seen people select and interpret information (cherry-pick evidence) that supports their existing beliefs. When they do, they are experiencing a **confirmatory bias**. In addition to making them more likely to believe something that doesn't contradict their existing beliefs, this bias also influences how much proof they need before they accept something that is counter to their beliefs. Similarly, the **Semmelweis reflex** causes us to reject evidence that conflicts with our existing beliefs.

Unlike confidence-building and self-centric biases, the **negativity bias** protects you by exaggerating negative aspects of situations. Imagine that two people hear a noise in the dark. One thinks nothing of it, while the other interprets the noise as a threat (a negative perception of the noise). If a predator made the noise, the person with the negativity bias, having prepared for the worst, is more likely to survive. If the noise was not made by a predator, the negativity bias might have wasted time and effort, but it would have no significant survival disadvantage. However, to the extent that this bias discourages taking action that might lead to success, it can be a disadvantage.

Did Nature bias your thinking to help you succeed by convincing others to agree with you? By causing you to selectively remember, interpret, or evaluate information non-consciously, the **motivated reasoning** bias enables you to get what you want by arguing with confidence, conviction, and with body language that convinces others to agree with you.[3]

When you think about something too frequently, you are likely to experience the **focusing illusion**. It causes you to perceive things you focus on excessively to be more important than they are. The illusion can be caused by repetitive rituals or group activities that require your group to hyper-focus on political, religious, academic, or other doctrines.

Do you believe that a part of you existed before you were born and will continue to exist after you die? These are pre-life and post-life **eternal existence biases**. Children who were not taught that a spirit-like part of them existed before they were born nonetheless believed that they existed in a pre-life form that was able to perceive emotions and desires.[4] Similarly, 40 studies in 20 countries found that many humans believe that a part of them continues to exist after they die. **This research concluded that theology or belief in the existence of a supernatural world results from a basic human impulse or bias that causes people to perceive themselves to have a dualistic nature where their spirit or mind survives their physical death.**[5, 6]

Brain traits

In addition to inheriting mental biases, **we inherit anatomical and biochemical "brain traits" that silently influence how our brains process information and, consequently, how we perceive reality.**

Intuitive and reflective memory

Our memory system evolved with two ways to remember, both without our conscious awareness. One is intuitive (also known as reflexive) and the other is reflective.[7]

Intuitive memory uses many experiences to form generalizations about those experiences. It is an averaging process that is slow to form and slow to change. For this reason, **your intuitive memories are relatively insensitive to the opinions of others, where such opinions represent just one experience.** When observing an event causes your intuitive memory to respond, you won't recall specific experiences that contributed to that intuitive memory. Instead, you will sense a feeling, intuition, impression, suspicion, hunch, or insight about the observed event.

Reflective memory is your other memory system and, unlike intuitive memories, reflective memories can form and change with just one experience. For this reason, your reflective memory is more influenced by the opinions of others. You rely on reflective memory when your intuitive memory hasn't had a sufficient number of experiences to form a generalized intuitive memory or when some condition requires that your reflective memory supersede your intuitive memory.

An example of how these memory systems work together would be when you park your car in the same place every day, but one day you park somewhere else. When you return to find your car, your intuitive memory will direct you to your usual parking place. **However, your reflective memory will override your intuitive memory to get you to your car.**[8] Another example of conflicting intuitive and reflective memories might occur if you are asked to name the color of a printed word, but not the color that the word spells. If the word *red* is written in blue ink, there's a habitual, intuitive tendency to read the word and respond with "red." To avoid this mistake, it is necessary for your brain to resolve the conflict by choosing your reflective memory response to provide the correct answer: "blue."[9]

How does your reflective memory override your intuitive memory? Researchers have found a brain region that compares predictions of intuitive and reflective memory systems. Their research suggests that this "arbitrator" region influences decision making by inhibiting

intuitive memory when the arbitrator determines that reflective memory is more likely to produce a desired outcome. This process returns the answer "blue" in the previous example.[10] However, it appears that some of us default to our intuitive memory because we are born insensitive to conflicts between our intuitive and reflective memories. That insensitivity inclines us to make decisions using our intuitive recollections.[11] The degree to which you are sensitive to intuitive/reflective memory conflicts is a brain trait.[12]

Reciprocal thinking regions

Our brains are structured with two separate but coordinated thinking regions. One region processes analytical thinking, while the other processes intuitive thinking. Analytical thinking is slow, deliberative, rule-governed, and primarily verbal. It uses reasoning instead of rules of thumb. Alternatively, intuitive thinking tends to rely on intuitive memory, which can result in our using rules of thumb. This kind of thinking is good when problems cannot be solved through analysis or in quick-response situations. It is fast, automatic, and all-inclusive. **While these thinking regions are separate, they coordinate such that when one region is activated the other is deactivated in a reciprocal inhibition relationship. This means that by beginning thinking with our intuitive thinking region, we will persist in thinking intuitively even if thinking analytically would**

be more appropriate, and vice versa.[13] In other words, if we begin using our intuitive thinking region in a fearful situation, we are not likely to analyze the situation rationally.

Our preference for using one or the other of these thinking regions depends on whether we are habitually inclined to think analytically or intuitively. Which thinking region we begin with is influenced by our sensitivity to intuitive/reflective memory conflicts and things such as urgency, complexity, and the situation's emotional content. [14,15,16]

Thinking styles

Numerous studies of twins in different countries over 20 years conclude that **we're born with a tendency toward conservative or liberal thinking styles. This means that whether we prefer risk-taking (associated with a liberal thinking style) or predictability (associated with a conservative thinking style) is significantly influenced by the genetic traits we inherit.**[17] Those of us who are insensitive to reflective/intuitive memory conflicts rely more on intuitive memories and tend to have a conservative thinking style, whereas those who are sensitive to reflective/intuitive memory conflicts tend to have a liberal thinking style. It's important to note that the liberal and conservative thinking styles described here don't refer to conservative or liberal political preferences.

Other characteristics of conservative and liberal thinking styles were made clear in a long-term study of children. The study found that children who developed close relationships were energetic, self-reliant, somewhat dominating, and resilient and had relatively low self-restraint; they were also more likely to become adults that were inclined to see things in an uncommon way and were frustrated by societal constraints. As adults, they relied less on intuitive thinking and tended to be more responsive to complexity and ambiguity; they were generally associated with flexible thinking, creativity, curiosity, and novelty-seeking.[18]

In that same study, children who tended to feel victimized were easily offended, indecisive, fearful, vulnerable, rigid, inhibited, and had relatively high self-restraint; were inclined to become adults with a more conservative thinking style. They were uncomfortable with uncertainty, comfortable with structure and predictability, and were resistant to change in established modes of behavior. They were attracted by and supported decisive leaders with a presumed ability to enhance security.

Why do some people prefer predictability, while others prefer to experience risk and change? Behavioral neuroscientists studied thinking styles in animals with brain structures similar to humans. They found that animals experiencing unpredictability had an elevated level of the protein gephyrin in the decision-making part of their brains. Other animal research has associated elevated gephyrin to a strong preference for order and certainty. This suggests that a high gephyrin level probably contributes to risk aversion, which in humans

is associated with a conservative thinking style. See endnote 19 for a more detailed description.

What effect do thinking styles have on how we solve problems? Research has shown that people with a liberal thinking style, after thinking about a problem, suddenly become aware of a solution. Conservative thinking style problem-solving tends to rely on intuitive feelings to arrive at a solution. **Numerous studies have come to the conclusion that those with a liberal thinking style have a less structured, more flexible problem-solving style, while those with a conservative thinking style tend to be more structured and persistent in solving problems.** That being said, regardless of their normal thinking style, people with either thinking style have the ability to use a deliberate problem-solving method using a gradual, methodical, analytical approach in which they are aware of the steps taken to arrive at the solution.[20]

What effect do neurotransmitters have on decision making? In stressful situations, the neurotransmitter noradrenaline increases attention, vigilance, and involuntary nervous system readiness—the flight-or-fight response. During that process, noradrenaline inhibits reflective memory, which is associated with a liberal thinking style. However, it has no effect on intuitive memory, which is associated with a conservative thinking style. In essence, the release of noradrenaline during a flight-or-fight response forces people with a liberal thinking style to rely more on their intuitive memory system, i.e., to think as if they had a conservative thinking style.

Priming

When a first experience predisposes you to perceive a later experience in a biased way, the priming brain trait is non-consciously altering how you perceive reality. In one example, seeing a photo of an injured bird followed by a photo of someone smiling will predispose you to perceive the person smiling as lacking empathy. The first photo primes your response to the second photo by inducing a narrative where none exists.

Apperception

We acquired our early beliefs when we were unable to assess the validity of what we were taught. What we learned as children reflected the beliefs of our parents, our religion, culture, peers, and others. Later in life, those early beliefs shape the way we see the world by influencing how we perceive new experiences. Psychologists refer to this brain trait as apperception. It is a process by which your new experiences are assimilated and transformed by your existing beliefs and understanding. This is different from confirmatory bias, which inclines us to confirm our existing beliefs. An example of apperception was seen when two people from religious and non-religious families encountered a vagrant asking for money. How did they respond? Apperception caused both to interpret their experience by transforming their perception of the vagrant to fit the

narrative of their existing beliefs. Unlike the non-religious narrative, the religious narrative was found to be judgmental rather than empathetic.[21] Inasmuch as apperception occurs non-consciously, **we are not aware that beliefs acquired earlier in life are altering how we perceive the world.**

Dysrationalia

Can our early beliefs prevent us from thinking rationally? Psychologist Keith Stanovich developed the concept of **dysrationalia**, which he describes as **an inability to think and behave rationally, and to have difficulty in forming beliefs and assessing belief consistency even with adequate intelligence.** Stanovich described a study of selected members of a high-IQ club (Mensa) in Canada to determine whether they believed in astrology and extraterrestrial visitors, neither of which is supported by scientific evidence. In their answers, 44 percent believed that astrology was real and 56 percent believed that the Earth has been visited by extraterrestrials.[22] It has been argued that Stanovich's dysrationalia concept lacks a theory that explains why people are dysrational and how they become that way. Presumably, the Mensa members who believed that astrology and extraterrestrial visitors are real were taught or came to believe these things earlier in their lives. **In my view, adequate intelligence can't always compensate for false early memories, and the reality-distorting apperceptions they create.** If evidence-based information and clear reasoning are necessary to reach valid conclusions, then believing that astrology and extraterrestrial visitors are real, no matter how good your reasoning, will result in dysrational thinking consistent with those beliefs.

Emotional vs. rational thinking

Before our ancestors were able to reason, their limbic brain (Appendix A) provided them with the emotion-based thinking they needed to survive and reproduce. In time, our ancestor's brains evolved to provide them with the additional ability to reason. **Today, both reason and emotional thinking control our actions.** Although this arrangement helps our continued survival, it presents a problem because our brain circuitry subordinates reason to the emotional thinking of our more primitive reptilian limbic system. By retaining the limbic system's extremely fast response to threats, we avoid the possibility that the act of reasoning might cause a delay that could threaten our survival. Imagine if pilots waited a few seconds for the prefrontal lobes of their neocortex to decide to avoid a midair collision. Instead, they respond almost instantly. In the 2009 water landing of a passenger plane on the Hudson River in New York City, Captain "Sully" Sullenberger made a series of rapid decisions without the benefit of time to analyze all the probabilities.

By overlaying our emotional brain regions with a neocortex, Nature gives us a second way to relate to the world. Daniel Goleman, in *Emotional Intelligence,* described how the limbic and neocortex systems coordinate to make decisions:

In a very real sense we have two minds, one that thinks and one that feels . . . These two minds, the emotional and the rational, operate in tight harmony for the most part, intertwining their very different ways of knowing to guide us through the world. In many or most moments these minds are exquisitely coordinated; feelings are essential to thought, thought to feeling. But when passions surge the balance tips: it is the emotional mind that captures the upper hand, swamping the rational mind.[23]

We are left with the realization that, once again, our genetic chaperones employ the Stone Age perceptions that kept our ancestors alive. Inasmuch as we no longer live in a Stone Age world, is reason more likely than prehistoric brain traits and biases to keep us alive today?

The planning assumption

We're born with an intentionality bias that causes us to perceive intent in the actions of others, even when there is none. By the time we're about one year old, this bias causes us to perceive goal-directed intentions in the actions of our parents and others.[28] This bias might have kept our ancestors alive by causing them to perceive actions or events to be the result of someone's intentional act. **Given our day-to-day experiences with planning, this bias can cause us to conclude that something was**

planned simply because "it appears to be the result of someone's intentional act."

During Darwin's time, a common planning assumption was that if something as complex as a watch has a watchmaker, then something as wondrous as the universe must have a creator. When you look at spectacular telescopic images of the universe, what does your intentionality bias tell you? Charles Darwin had to confront the planning assumption if *On the Origin of Species by Way of Natural Selection* was to be understood and accepted. In it he wrote on the first page of Chapter XV:

> Nothing at first can appear more difficult to believe than that the more complex organs and instincts should have been perfected not by means superior to, though analogous with, human reason [planning], but by the accumulation of innumerable slight variations [beneficial random mutations], each good for the individual possessor.

While we might see ourselves as part of an intentionally planned cosmos, Darwin was telling us that the simple process of trial and error selection—without intention, understanding, intelligence, or planning—evolved humans and other lifeforms.

Conspiracy theories

To varying degrees, we inherited the ability to detect social conspiracies. We are able to perceive certain patterns, recognize when others are exercising control, and perceive

hidden alliances. We use rules of thumb, intuitions, and emotions to process these perceptions. In addition, certain social and other factors correlate with our being inclined to see conspiracies. A few examples are having poor analytical thinking skills; having a strong in-group identity while being involved with a powerful out-group; being part of a collectively narcissistic group; being inclined to fearfulness, paranoia, or schizophrenia; tending to be socially or politically withdrawn; having feelings of alienation; or having extreme ideological beliefs. In essence, the degree to which we are inclined to see conspiracies depends on the genetic chaperones and mental predispositions we inherit as well as beliefs we acquire about ourselves and our groups.

The widespread tendency of early humans to believe conspiracy theories is thought to have better adapted them to survive against powerful and potentially hostile coalitions. Today, however, our ability to perceive conspiracies can be orchestrated intentionally to direct suspicion against specific groups. This has been observed in groups involved with political extremism, populism, and religious fundamentalism. More specifically, conspiracy theories are thought to function as "radicalizing multipliers" in the internal workings of such groups.[24]

Groupthink

Groupthink is an example of how inborn brain traits and biases combine in a way that,

in this case, benefits the survival of tribes and social groups. Given events that began with 9/11, specific examples are provided to make clear how the nature of extreme groupthink is used to concentrate power.

In *The Science of Fear*, Daniel Gardner wrote:

> **We are social animals and what others think matters deeply to us. The group's opinion isn't everything; we can buck the trend. But even when the other people involved are strangers, even when we are anonymous, even when dissenting will cost us nothing, we want to agree with the group.**[25]

Societies organize by using hierarchies based on wealth, age, sex, religion, ethnicity, and things such as liberal or conservative thinking styles. **We inherit the tendency to believe that social hierarchies are justified, and children as young as five years of age are able to understand their association with and the status of their group. They are motivated to favor their group and are inclined to defend the status quo.**[26] As members of an in-group, we see ourselves positively, with an enhanced sense of self-esteem and social value. **We view our group positively, with a sense of group self-esteem, and we stereotype and attribute negative characteristics to out-groups.** The following article by John R. Alford and John R. Hibbing in *Perspectives on Politics* describes typical groupthink behaviors:

1. Cooperate with others in the group.
2. Dislike those in out-groups.
3. Punish or banish uncooperative in-group members.
4. Encourage others through norms, institutions, or moral codes to follow 1, 2, and 3.
5. Be sensitive to status, inducements, and reputation relative to other in-group members.
6. Cease cooperating if the non-cooperation of other members goes unpunished.[27]

As part of an "in-group," we tend to rely on the decisions of other group members. If many of us do this, our group focuses more on each other and less on outside influences. By relying too much on influential group members, those with less influence can experience a conflict between their individual interests and the group's interests. If that conflict becomes unacceptable, members are not prevented from leaving the group.

Unlike normal groupthink, extreme groupthink occurs when group members experience a very strong desire for group harmony or conformity. This motivates members to minimize group conflict by suppressing dissenting opinions and by refusing to consider outside opinions. This creates biased analytical thinking that can be irrational or dysrational. Loyalty, which can be enforced by "mind-guards", is shown by avoiding controversy. Unanimity created by these behaviors creates an artificial sense of rightness in the group's decision making, and creates an "illusion of invulnerability." The drive for harmony exaggerates the group's sense of its abilities and underestimates the abilities of out-groups.

At least some of those who are inclined to **extreme groupthink are what the futurist Eric Hoffer describes as "true believers." They believe themselves incapable of self-direction and are insecure joiners and followers who want to be told what to believe. True believers make perfect followers in politics, business, social causes, and organized religions and are ideal candidates to be made into zealots by charismatic leaders.** The danger posed by zealots was noted by Louis D. Brandeis (1856–1941), associate justice of the U.S. Supreme Court: "The greatest dangers to liberty lurk in insidious encroachment by men of zeal, well-meaning but without understanding."

If we prohibit falsely shouting "Fire!" in a crowded theater, how should we treat inflammatory words spoken to an audience of zealots or robotized followers? How should we view words that would not move an ordinary person to violence, but would be considered a command by a zealot? Are zealots with little independent thinking a weapon of the speaker controlling them? Should leaders of zealots and robotized followers be prevented from using incitement speech? If so, who among us will decide when such speech rises to the level of incitement to violence in cases such as bombing abortion clinics or in killing innocent people because religious leaders believe they have a right not to be offended by those who exercise their right to free speech.

Extreme groupthink members gain self-esteem, security, and a sense of identity and control that they don't experience on their own, especially if they have low self-esteem and low assertiveness. Group cohesiveness, however, makes members susceptible to peer pressure to conform, makes them likely to self-censor their ideas to match the group consensus and encourages them to forego conflicting personal beliefs and values. This way of thinking closes their minds to outside information that doesn't conform to group beliefs and thereby reinforces the group's way of seeing the world. By vilifying and preventing contact with people from other groups, their way of seeing the world is insulated from contradiction.[28]

Extreme groupthink organizations can inflate the importance of their beliefs by using the focusing illusion. To do this, all aspects of group life are permeated with extreme groupthink ideology by using repetitious rituals, authoritarian directives, extensive focus on approved beliefs, excessive regulation of members' personal conduct, and the organizing of group activities and events. This causes members to perceive their beliefs as having exaggerated importance. Our history appears to be rife with the result of this kind of groupthink-focusing illusion. In extreme groupthink organizations, has thinking distorted by the focusing illusion been responsible for sectarian wars, the Inquisitions, Nazi atrocities, and present Jihadist terrorism?

Extreme groupthink creates flawed decisions based on logical fallacies such as arguing that things are true based on authority, tradition, oversimplification, stereotyping, guilt by association, half-truths, and the declaration that their views are sacrosanct. Even if extreme groupthink organizations are small, they can control large populations by using force, propaganda, social media, and fake news to manipulate the public's genetic chaperones. We saw this when Nazi party groupthink members carefully crafted propaganda to cause millions of people to condone dehumanizing bigotry, which resulted in the mass killing of Jews, gypsies, mental patients, and others. It is said that Hitler's propaganda minister, Joseph Goebbels, kept a copy of Edward Bernays' propaganda classic *Crystallizing Public Opinion* on his desk (see Appendix B).

Through the ages, various leaders have used extreme groupthink to ensure compliance with their political and religious doctrines. When extreme groupthink is used, the group's leaders create robotized followers who are conditioned not to think for themselves, not to ask questions, and to mindlessly endorse group beliefs and follow orders. **Today, members of such groups are referred to as "sheeple."**

Extreme groupthink religious education can produce easily controlled "robotized" followers who can be converted to follow the ideology of power-seeking leaders. Today, extreme groupthink leaders use social media and the internet to spread a message of community and empowerment to the poor, the socially or religiously polarized, the alienated, those with low self-esteem, religious zealots, educated sheeple, and those experiencing hopelessness, religious discrimination, and despair.

In this chapter, we examined what genetic chaperones are, why we have them, and how their brain traits and biases create fictitious perceptions to aid survival. While their genetic chaperones provided our ancestors with a survival advantage, the disadvantage was that the beliefs they formed were based on fiction and not reality. The connection between their

DNA and the fictitious beliefs they created is symbolized on the cover of this book. It shows an upper spiral of DNA that creates fictitious beliefs that are recorded in the lower spiral stack of books. The symbolism of that relationship begs the question, if we know that fictitious perceptions shaped many of our beliefs, do we have an obligation to avoid passing them on to future generations?

Chapter 3

How genetic chaperones influence belief formation and cultural evolution

To understand where we are going, it is helpful to know where we have been. Not long ago, our ancestors lived in Stone Age groups that gradually grew in size and complexity. Their accumulated perceptions of the world began to coalesce into early cultures. Those early cultures evolved into the cultures we see today, which raises the question, by what process do cultures evolve?

Relatively recently, when Charles Darwin explained the process of genetic evolution, people wondered whether cultural evolution evolved in a way similar to genetic evolution. They speculated that cultural evolution involved gene like "units of culture" that passed from person to person. A few described units of culture as actimes, mnemes, mentifacts, and memones. In his book *The Selfish Gene*, Dr. Richard Dawkins proposed the word "meme." While I understand that Dr. Dawkins' view of memes has changed somewhat, in his book, he categorized them as things such as tunes, ideas, and catch-phrases. **He described memes as passing from person to person by a parasitizing viral transmission process or by an imitative process of "catching on." [1]**

For a belief transmission theory to be convincing, it should provide a plausible description of the process. In addition, scientific theories (hypotheses) generally require that the theory be validated by experiment. If units of culture are transmitted from person to person by virus/host transmission or by imitation, what are the processes that accomplish transmission? **My hypothesis is that units of culture are simply "beliefs" that people have about what is real, appropriate, have value, are true, exist or do not exist, are ways of doing things, and the like. Belief transmission begins when someone's belief is made know or proffered to one or more potential recipients. If a potential recipient perceives the proffered belief to have "acquisition value," that unit of culture will be accepted and belief transmission will take place. The recipient's perception of acquisition value need not be analytical or even conscious. It might result from a strong, immediate desire to acquire the proffered belief. Our cultures are belief systems that we and our ancestors assembled by this process,** and cultural differences reflect differences in our belief systems.

To simplify discussing belief transmission in this way, I use the term "psychogenetic" transmission. It derives from the word

"psychogene"[2], which comprises a belief component (psycho) and a (gene)-like transmission component, both of which are involved in transmitting a belief from person to person.

In essence, a "psychogene" is a belief that is "made known" or "proffered" to a potential recipient. Such proffers can be by direct communication between people or by indirect communication such as via the internet, television, email, books, social media, and the like. Whether we acquire a direct or indirect proffer depends on factors such as our habitual patterns of behavior and how our brains process thoughts and emotions. Once accepted, the belief is available to be proffered to others. It seems clear that this process of psychogenetic transmission fits Dr. Dawkins' description of a meme "catching on." My view is that memes that "go viral" are psychogenes that are quickly accepted and reproffered to many people in a short time.

Is it possible to predict whether a proffered psychogene will be acquired? That depends on how clearly we understand a potential recipient's perception of its acquisition value. Knowing how people perceive value is the focus of behavioral and social scientists. They study how we make decisions by considering things such as peer recommendations, social status, need satisfaction, the effects of fads, imitation behavior (monkey see, monkey do), and the way marketing and advertising strategies are used to bias our decision making. Additional influences include maturity, aging, personality disorders, mental aberrations, addictions, and other factors. Appendix B describes how public relations experts can use propaganda techniques to manipulate our genetic chaperone's biases and brain traits to influence how we perceive acquisition value. This means that **our genetic chaperone's survival enhancing false perceptions are central to the process of cultural evolution. By influencing our perceptions of acquisition value, genetic chaperone biases that cause us to perceive conspiracy theories, illusory correlations, and the like, have shaped the way our cultures have evolved.**

How does psychogenetic transmission take place with children whose belief systems are in the process of being formed? To survive in our ancestors' world, children needed to acquire knowledge quickly. To this end, Nature evolved a childhood period of "suggestibility." During that period, children acquire beliefs on blind faith from authority figures and others whose endorsement gives acquisition value to their proffered beliefs. This process enables children to acquire a river of beliefs about real and imaginary things that their developing belief systems cannot evaluate. **As they grow older, their apperception brain trait causes them to assimilate and transform new experiences consistent with the narrative of their existing beliefs. Similarly, they might reject proffered beliefs because they conflict with their existing beliefs (the Semmelweis reflex). While these biases benefited our Stone Age ancestors, today, to the extent that apperception and the Semmelweis reflex**

prevent us from acquiring new beliefs or changing existing beliefs, these biases can irreversibly limit our ability to adapt to new situations. Another concern is that, unlike genetic evolution that acquires genetic "knowledge" from countless ancestral trial and error survival experiences, our belief systems can acquire and organize beliefs regardless of reality. **We can find acquisition value in psychogenes because of our genetic chaperone's false perceptions. And when we do, our belief systems simply organize ignorance.**

For beliefs to survive over successive generations, they must experience a continuous chain of psychogenetic transmissions. For this reason, core beliefs, which are relevant to every generation, are retransmitted by each generation. While this causes our core beliefs to persist, beliefs perceived to lack proffer value because they are outdated or are no longer meaningful, are less likely to persist for lack of retransmission.

Understanding the influence genetic chaperones have on how our beliefs form and how our cultures evolve should provide us with a clearer understanding of reality. With that understanding, we should be less vulnerable to manipulation by propagandists and more likely to recognize our genetic chaperone's false perceptions.

Chapter 4

The origin of belief systems

It's not possible to know with certainty what our ancestors thought as they evolved from nomadic makers of stone tools into artisans with a rudimentary vocabulary, rock and cave paintings, agriculture, and domesticated animals. However, **archeological findings and studies of contemporary primitive cultures might provide a glimpse into the influences that shaped our ancestors' belief systems.**

How did our ancient ancestors perceive their world?

Imagine the year is 80,000 BCE, and you are one of your ancestors. You find yourself in a world of which you are profoundly ignorant. Death, disease, and fertility are mysterious. Your world is a confusing and dangerous place. Many years before you were born, your ancestors began to create language and to understand that others have different beliefs, intentions, perspectives, and desires. With language and understanding, you discuss a spirit world in addition to the one you see around you. You separate your material and spirit worlds with increasingly sophisticated myths as you perceive your dreams to be a window into your spirit world. When you eat certain plants you hallucinate, which you believe is a spirit-world experience. You believe that your tribal shaman, a medium between the visible world and your invisible spirit world, explains your dreams, predicts or controls natural events, and heals the sick. You observe flowers that move to face the sun as it crosses the sky. You believe that plants, trees, animals, and natural events have a human-like consciousness and spirituality. You decorate your weapons with the images of the animals you hunt because you believe the images capture the animals' spirits and give you power over your prey. You treat the animals you kill and the trees you cut with respect because you believe the spirits of all things are interconnected. You worship the spirits of your dead ancestors. Members of your tribe eat the bodies of slain enemies to obtain the power of their spirits. Your parents, who protected you in youth, are now dead, and in their place you believe that parent and ancestor spirits protect you. For spiritual protection, you offer barter in the form of offerings, prayers, sacrifices, and rituals.

You think in simple symbolic form, which contributes to your lack of distinction between the real and spirit worlds. As your speaking skills increase in precision and complexity you begin to separate the material and spirit worlds with more sophisticated myths. You observe that celestial cycles are related to weather and life cycles on Earth, and you conclude that celestial spirits control the stars, the weather, life on Earth, and all things in the universe. As winter progresses, the sun moves lower in the sky and you believe that evil spirits are threatening you. You aren't sure if the sun will continue to descend and eventually drop below the horizon, never to return. You are elated at the winter solstice, when the sun reverses course and warmth and life begin to return to your world.

You interpret eclipses as celestial dragons attempting to devour the sun and moon, and you prevent those disasters by using dances and rituals to barter with your spirits. You record lunar, solar, and celestial cycles in stone circles, and by cutting marks on bones. Your shaman discovered the trance-inducing effects of certain plants and thought it a gift from one of your animal spirits.

Before about 50,000 years ago, when you began to paint on cave walls, humans experienced a testosterone mutation that made males less aggressive, more agreeable, and more able to learn from interacting with others. They tended to have a rounder skull and a much less prominent brow ridge.[1] Increased agreeableness improved cooperation in tool making, art, and exchanging beliefs with other group members.

Some of your wall paintings use pigments bound together with the marrow of animals depicted in the paintings. Some paintings show the trance-inducing plants. Others show geometric designs commonly seen during drug-induced hallucinations. The creation myth you create comprises a narrative consistent with things specific to your environment and your understanding of Nature. **Eventually your mythological spirits (bodiless animal analogs) evolve into various omnipotent, immortal gods with animal forms, possessing supernatural power that can relieve your suffering, ensure fertility, and steel you against the forces of Nature. All this you believe**

without question and, most fundamentally, you believe that a bodiless intelligence animates the universe. You and your fellow humans have become animists. In his poem, *Evolution*, Langdon Smith (1858–1908) described this period of transition in human history:

> The shadows broke and the soul awoke
> In a strange, dim dream of God.

Lest we look at these ancestral beliefs condescendingly, we should be mindful of a few things. Our ancestors managed their fears, lived in balance with Nature, and survived to make our generation possible. Could it be that the modern soul derives from their concept of a personal spirit, and that modern gods evolved from inherited beliefs about spirits? It's obvious that modern religions did not spontaneously generate. With their similar fundamental concepts, it seems apparent that today's religions evolved from our ancestors' animistic beliefs and their understanding of Nature.

By the time ancient Greek civilization peaked, our ancestors' primary focus shifted from creation myths that supported gods in animal form to creation myths that supported gods that looked like us. This evolution was so complete by the 16ᵗʰ century that European Christians debated whether the natives they encountered in the Americas were actually humans. Michelangelo Buonarroti (1475–1564) cast his vote in favor of their being fellow humans when he painted them into the human family as part of his work in the Sistine Chapel. What European Christians found in the

Americas were cousins whose mythology, unlike their own, had not evolved much beyond the animism of their Eurasian ancestors. In a way, Europeans stood face to face with their ancestors and didn't recognize them.

Animism and modern religions are useful to the extent that they enable their believers to cope with the difficulties of life. The price for this usefulness, however, is measured in the damage that results from their conflict with reality and from the sacrifice, ostracism, and hostility that flow from a need many have to deny the validity of the contrary beliefs of others.

My attempt to reconstruct the origins of mythology addresses certain timeless human and natural factors that influence myth creation. It seems apparent that fertility, adversity, disease, community, death, ignorance, mystery, fear, dreams, intuition, and our perception-altering genetic chaperones have all shaped our myths. It also seems apparent that every culture has a need to explain how our universe was created, and those myriad explanations are culture-specific and have evolved over thousands of years into the revered and immutable beliefs we hold today. Perhaps the only reality to be found in all of this is that those creation myths can't all be right, but they can all be wrong.

Did dreams and hallucinations shape early myths?

What do dreams have to do with myths? **If a dream can create the same emotional response as a real experience, why wouldn't a primitive mind think that dreams are real? If they did, it would explain the dream-like, magical, and non-physical aspects of their mythologies.** In addition to dreams, hallucinations are dream-like states that can be achieved through various means including meditation, rhythmic rituals, certain drugs, sensory deprivation, fasting, and fatigue. Hallucinations result from disrupting the normal flow of neural impulses in the brain. For example, eating mushrooms containing psilocin can disrupt the thalamus, the part of the forebrain that relays sensory impulses to the prefrontal lobes where thought, reasoning, and memory are processed. Once disrupted, the thalamus excessively passes sensory impulses to the prefrontal lobes, causing us to perceive artificial experiences (hallucinations.) When such mushrooms are used in a religious context, the hallucination becomes a transcendent experience.

Joseph Campbell (1904–1987) described dreams as personalized myths that reflect the dreamer's unique situation. Myths, on the other hand, are dreams that are not personalized, but are generally true for a given group.[3] In my view, myths provide us with a sense of control over the essentials of life and with peace of mind through "understanding" our world. They connect us with immortality and, in some cases, with a supernatural parent or guardian capable of protecting us. Myths frighten some of us into socially acceptable behavior that conforms our individual needs to those of our group. For some, even if our myths disappoint us, it might be easier to believe an otherwise supportive myth than to accept uncertainty or an unpleasant reality.

The fears that influenced our ancestors' myths originate in almond-shaped masses (amygdalae) in the front portion of the brain's temporal lobes. While fear clearly has survival value, too much fear can paralyze, while too little fear can imperil. Too little fear is apparently not the concern of myth. It appears that a benefit of myth is that it encourages us to persevere in the face of fear. To the extent that myth can remove fear, it empowers us to overcome adversity and provides us with a survival advantage. Otherwise stated, fear aids in creating myths that strengthen us against the thing we fear. The promise of eternal, idyllic life can transform into confident optimists those who might otherwise see life as an endless fear of dying. Chapter 5 describes how Emperor Constantine and Church leaders in Rome both used this aspect of mythology to their advantage. Constantine's mostly Christian army fought with confidence and religious fervor, winning battles that made Constantine the emperor of both the Eastern and Western Roman Empires. And, by cooperating with Constantine, Church leaders achieved their goal of establishing Roman Christianity as the religion of the Western Roman Empire.

By combining mysticism and practical beliefs in parables and symbolic forms, our ancestors' magical thinking conveyed the essence of the spiritual aspects of our cultures from generation to generation. Whether centered on trees, animals, or supernatural parents, they gave meaning to the lives of many and, to varying degrees, have given us comforting and useful imagined control over the world in which we find ourselves. *The Encyclopedia of Psychology* describes the origins of magical thought common to myths:

> Although modern society places great emphasis on the importance of rational thinking, research suggests that human beings today are as prone to magical thought as were their primitive ancestors. There seems to be a universal inclination to infer symbolic and meaningful relationships among objects and events, and an inability or a disinclination [unwillingness] to properly evaluate the experiences upon which these inferences are based [illusory correlations] . . . While occultisms reflect an attempt, through magical thinking, to understand the workings of Nature, they operate by and large outside conscious awareness, and often may serve the needs to increase personal power and to find solace in the face of existential anxiety [fear] . . . It is unlikely that human beings will ever be free of such needs or of the propensity for magical thought. Occultisms will in all likelihood always be with us in one guise or another, waxing [increasing] when social organization is undergoing rapid change leading to widespread anxiety, and waning [decreasing] during periods of social stability.[3]

Whether from magical thinking, dreams, hallucinations, or the biases and traits of our

genetic chaperones, it appears that beliefs based on imagined realities add illusory narratives to our belief systems. Given that such narratives are created from the mistaken or illusory beliefs of which their creators were unaware, they represent organized ignorance. Animism, for example, relies on beliefs about magical spirits, which form a coherent and organized narrative. After learning these narratives, as we age, our apperception, Semmelweis reflex, and dysrationalia can prevent us from accepting beliefs contrary to these early narratives. In this way, those narratives can become irreversible.

What is belief persistence?

An essential requirement of any culture is that its core beliefs are passed from one generation to the next. While core beliefs define and perpetuate our cultures, changing circumstances can necessitate adapting our beliefs to conform to our current understanding of reality. For example, we are now aware of bacteria and viruses and no longer attribute disease to being cursed.

Each of us learns our culture's core beliefs before we are experienced enough to evaluate them. This can result in our passing on beliefs that might be incorrect in light of what has been learned since the beliefs were originally created. In fundamentalist cultures, this faithful passing on of beliefs without alteration is a central tenet of the culture. And when adults unquestioningly pass on their unaltered childhood beliefs to their children, in effect they are children teaching

children. In so doing, inherited beliefs do not benefit from knowledge that has come to light in the years since those childhood beliefs originated. This appears to be why some fundamentalist belief systems reject new knowledge, such as how biological evolution works and the prior existence of dinosaurs. It is a kind of cultural bubble inside of which each generation is born.

Unfortunately, many of the ancestors who created the core beliefs we inherited were people who didn't know where the sun goes at night, that children are the result of sexual intercourse, and that the Earth isn't the center of the universe. **Consequently, we inherited many beliefs that combine to form a model of reality that is inaccurate or simply wrong.** It is entirely possible that, if the ancestors who created such beliefs had the knowledge we have today, they wouldn't have created them. **Even though history shows that ancestral beliefs can evolve over time, the belief transmission problem of children teaching children makes altering inherited beliefs difficult and such belief systems persistent. When we acquire beliefs during our period of suggestibility and thereafter, what we become reflects those beliefs. As adults, we protect our core beliefs because they have become "self", and any challenge to our core beliefs is a challenge to us personally.**

Since our young are highly suggestible and are biologically inclined to learn on blind faith, they inherit beliefs from authority figures whose endorsement gives those beliefs acquisition value. In addition, reward, shame, repetition, threats, and the social influence of religious, political, and peer leaders perpetuate our beliefs quite effectively. The Irish author and playwright George Bernard Shaw (1856–1950) wrote that children should pursue knowledge and not the other way around.[4]

Some Austrians include winter solstice demons of darkness in their celebration of Christmas. Pre-Christian celebrations of the winter solstice (when winter days begin to grow longer) result from memories of prehistoric hardship and of the joy their ancestors felt knowing that winter would soon end. Holding on to rituals, the meanings of which have been long forgotten, is a measure of the strength of belief persistence. It's as if these beliefs become separated from the reasons they were created and later take on a life of their own in the matrix of our cultural beliefs.

Given the persistence of beliefs, it is easier to redirect them than to terminate them. For this reason, instead of eliminating them, missionaries have converted native rituals and celebrations to their own use. To wit, in 601, Pope Gregory I instructed his missionaries not to destroy pre-Christian temples, but to destroy and replace their idols with Christian symbols. He instructed that religious feasts should continue, but the Christian God would be the new focus of those newly converted to Christianity.[5] Celebration of Christ's birthday began in the 5th century on the day of the winter solstice.[6] The celebration of Easter (Christ's resurrection) began in the 2nd century on the day Germanic pre-Christians celebrated Eostre (the goddess of spring) and when Jews celebrated Passover.

While beliefs define and perpetuate our cultures, some can be problematic. Even though, in great part, our knowledge of the things of life is greater than that of our ancestors, we typically assume that our ancestors' beliefs are valid and

accept them without challenge, and often with reverence. Our ancestors' unchallengeable beliefs, fashioned to satisfy the needs and biases of people long dead, reach into the future where they might serve a fitting purpose, or perhaps cause great harm. To compound this difficulty, religious leaders have incomes based on ensuring that each new generation acquires our ancestors' beliefs.

While we acquire new beliefs based on our perception of their acquisition value, there are circumstances where we acquire beliefs non-consciously. Research shows that things like acceptable baby names and codes of conduct can emerge spontaneously in a social network without a leader, organization, or publication to encourage their acceptance. For example, the name "Aiden" was once ranked 324th on a list of popular baby names. Fifteen years later it rose to the top 20 and has remained there for five years. This kind of non-conscious selection happens when people network on social media and are not aware that they are coordinating with each other. The mathematical model that predicted this result is called symmetry-breaking or the butterfly effect. It happens when small, undetectable changes spontaneously organize systems such as social networks to create a new stable state in the network.[7]

How belief systems organize ignorance

Considering the short time humans have existed in a universe that is billions of years old, it is clear that reality is what it is regardless of what we think it is. We organize what we believe reality to be into belief systems that contain the "truths" of our time. If our beliefs about reality fail to actually conform with or predict reality, it indicates that our beliefs about reality are invalid. If we put aside what we want reality to be and test our beliefs to eliminate personal or other biases, we are more likely to perceive reality as it is. Exposing our beliefs to rational criticism based on evidence is an excellent way to test beliefs. This is what scientists do every day, and their models of reality have been refined well enough for us to predict election results, fly safely to distant places, and expect to be cured using medical methods and equipment such as MRI machines.

One example of fake reality belief systems occurred during 1636 and 1637. At that time a large part of the Netherlands' population believed that tulips were so valuable that the price spiraled upwards as they outbid each other for tulips and tulip futures. It was called the tulip bubble. Eventually, when prices collapsed, many were badly damaged financially.

A more recent example is the dot-com bubble. In the late 1990s, new internet companies used their company name followed by ".com" to create their internet address. The dot-com bubble formed when the public bought stock in new internet companies with the expectation that they would revolutionize the way business is done. However, many of these companies lacked the business experience needed to turn ideas into profits. Investor excitement drove share prices to unrealistic levels. The dot-com bubble burst and millions of dollars were lost when public investors realized that most of the companies they had invested in would never make a profit.

The tulip and dot-com bubbles are examples of organized ignorance. While a bubble exists, those inside the bubble can't see it for what it is. One way of understanding these events is to think of each of us as having our own bubble of illusory beliefs, perhaps similar to beliefs held by people in the tulip or dot-com bubbles. If the beliefs of our personal bubbles are not commonly held, they are not cross-validating. However, if significant numbers of us were to believe the same unreality, our individual bubbles would combine to form a cross-validating bubble reality based on organized ignorance. As the internet makes it easier for us to find others of a similar mind, for the first time in history it is making possible the formation of cyber bubble realities of religious, political, and other extremists. Recent examples are jihadi and evangelizing groups that use the internet to recruit followers.

Whether a bubble will burst depends on the nature of the believed unreality. Financial bubbles burst because economic reality is material and must balance in the end. Metaphysical, intangible, or non-physical bubbles, by their nature, are not directly subject to objective accountability and can survive indefinitely, or until some consequence of their unreality bursts them. The Salem witch trials are an example of a metaphysical bubble. In this case, commonly held biblical beliefs about witches were the basis for a mass delusion that witches were present in their community. The trials began when young girls claimed to have been possessed by the devil due to the witchcraft of local women. Over 150 women were accused, and the resulting hysteria caused the formation of a special court. Nineteen were judged to be witches and were hanged. It is said that the bubble ended when respected citizens were accused of being witches.

Our genetic chaperones alter our perceptions of reality to promote behaviors likely to help us survive and endure. When those altered perceptions cause us to believe that reality is different from what it is, we add incorrect beliefs (ignorance) to our belief systems. Even though cultures might understand that the beliefs they inherited contain organized ignorance, they might be unable to adapt their belief systems to reflect reality, even if the organized ignorance threatens their cultural survival. If adapting to the changing world requires actions that conflict with traditional beliefs or with the beliefs of those in power, change will take place slowly, if at all. As rational as we think our beliefs are, it is likely that our belief systems contain arbitrary beliefs that will survive so long as they are not changed by rational understanding or otherwise.

Chapter 5

Belief system evolution

Over time, by altering the way our Eurasian ancestors perceived reality, their genetic chaperones gradually shaped their belief systems and contributed to what we know today as Western history.

Given the time it takes for belief systems to change, this chapter examines just over 2,000 years of Italian psychogenetic evolution. It begins with the Roman Republic (circa 8th to 1st century BCE), continues through the merger of Greek and Roman beliefs, through the gradually increasing influence of the Roman Christian Church (circa 1st to 4th century), and ends with the Italian Renaissance or rebirth of Greco–Roman cultural influences (circa 15th century). As this chapter describes belief system evolution, it recounts how philosophers tried to explain and deal with the same fundamental questions of life we face today. We find ourselves in a universe and don't know why it exists, whether it is limitless with no beginning or end, or whether an intelligent force created it. We wonder what we are, whether we have a purpose, whether we have a personal spirit that lived before and will live after our present existence, whether our future is predetermined, and what rules or concepts should guide us as we live our lives. For thousands of years, our ancestors pondered these questions. Their conflicting schools of thought between mythological and reasoned thinking reveal the convoluted paths our ancestors took with the aid of their ever-present and undetected genetic chaperones. It is a story of how competing ideas about the nature of reality shaped the thinking of their time. **Lest you think that revisiting 2,000 years of Western history has no relevance today, consider that the thinking of those ancestors lives on in our belief systems and is influencing how we see reality today.**

This chapter is neither intended to judge the accomplishments and failures of the people, governments, and institutions involved nor to favor one interpretation of history over another. That said, it is helpful to remember that a great deal of history is revealed in criticisms from people who were expressing their opposing beliefs and interests. Given that it is the only religion that significantly influenced the evolution of Western culture during the two millennia we will consider, the thinking of Roman Catholic philosophers is discussed in some detail.

Early Roman psychogenes

In about 753 BCE, the city of Rome began as a small town in central Italy about 20 miles from the sea. In time, its citizens formed a Republic, not a dictatorship. Citizens were serious, austere, and disciplined. Eugen Weber of the University of California at Berkeley described the core transmitted beliefs of the early Roman Republic as follows:

> The virtues the Romans admired were all related to discipline and self-discipline. They believed in "Pietas" – respect for established

authority and tradition. They believed in
"Fides" – being true to your responsibilities;
in "Religio" – the common belief[s] that bind
men together; and above all in "Gravitas" –
the sober seriousness that marks a real man.
Even the word "Virtus" means manliness . . .
True virtue subordinates the person to the
city, the individual to the state . . . The
Romans were a conservative people, and so
they wanted strong leaders, but not too
strong.[1]

Given that their time was one in which the law of force
and not the force of law governed tribal relationships,
the importance of discipline, authority, tradition, and
gravitas suggest that reliance on leaders with a
conservative thinking style was considered essential.

Armed with Pietas, Fides, Religio, and Gravitas,
they examined their world and gradually conquered it.
In the process, Roman ways of doing things changed
the agriculture, settlement patterns, and economics of
conquered lands. Formerly independent regions
conformed to the Roman model. Large farming estates
replaced smaller farmsteads. Roman economic and
military considerations dislocated populations and
influenced their belief systems. Change created wealth
for some, and new tax burdens for others. As with
assimilation at other times in human history, old
boundaries, beliefs, traditions, and cultural identities
were transformed as the Republic expanded.[2]

Rome acquires
Ancient Greek psychogenes

While the Republic was expanding, Roman culture itself was evolving. By conquering Greece in 146 BCE, the austere, militant Roman Republic took into its culture a psychogenetic Trojan horse. With Greece came Greek culture, which had been influenced by older cultures, including those of Egypt, Phoenicia, Judea, Crete, India, and Babylonia. The Roman statesman and philosopher Marcus Tullius Cicero (106–43 BCE) observed that "It was no little brook that flowed from Greece into our city, but a mighty river of culture and learning."[3]

Just prior to the Roman Republic's assimilation of Greece, the Axial Age had ended in Greece. In different countries across much of Eurasia, from about 800 to 200 BCE, an emergence of intellectually sophisticated thinking created formative concepts in literature, art, philosophy, and theology. We know this period for having produced the Hebrew Scriptures and the writings of the Ancient Greeks, Confucius, Laozi, and Buddha, among others. The period has been named the Axial Age for its pivotal introduction of an intellectually complex examination of human existence, natural occurrences, and the creation of the concept of transcendence. Axial Age thinkers profoundly influenced the thinking of subsequent cultures, philosophies, and religions, including those of the Roman Republic. To the extent that Greek learning and mythology reflected a liberal thinking style that was more responsive to complexity, ambiguity, flexible thinking, creativity, curiosity, and novelty seeking, assimilating Greek culture diluted austere Roman values.

Within about one hundred years after conquering Greece, Rome had been influenced significantly by the experience. As the Roman State assimilated its Greek gifts, Roman psychogenes evolved into Greco–Roman psychogenes, leaving behind the austere beliefs that fostered the Republic. This Greek psychogenetic inheritance contributed to the disengagement of the militaristic engine that drove the Roman Republic. Austere Roman gods were replaced by enlightened and self-indulgent Greek gods. With the strength of the Roman State rooted in a combination of mythology, superstition, nationalism, and self-discipline, these changes altered core Roman beliefs. With the increasing assimilation of Greek psychogenes, the Roman government could no longer appeal to the Pietas and Fides of its citizens. Instead, it relied on their fears, superstitions, and myths. With wealth and governmental power concentrating in the power elite, the austere psychogenetic inheritance of the Roman Republic's creators found fewer and fewer adherents. The tribune Sallust (c.86–c.34 BCE) observed the change in values in the first century BCE.[4] The values of personal responsibility, sober seriousness, self-discipline, tradition, and respect for authority were supplanted by greed, avarice, arrogance, and impiety.

The transition of the Roman Republic to a dictatorship was complex and will be represented briefly in this chapter by the fate of Tiberius and Gaius Gracchus, and the rise to power of Julius Caesar. While the Senate was making decisions driven by a desire to concentrate power and wealth in the hands of a few, it was alienating its citizens and was becoming accountable only to itself. Power had been concentrated in a limited number of elite families, and the constant battles for wealth and power eventually took their toll. **An attempt was made in the late 2nd century BCE, by Senate tribunes Tiberius and Gaius Gracchus, to pass land reform and other legislation to benefit the urban poor and veterans. The Gracchi's early successes lead to their deaths at the hands of their enemies in the Senate. Decades later, Julius Caesar, after a successful campaign in Gaul, returned to Rome and in time, was declared Dictator of the Roman Republic. He instituted land reform and other policies that angered Roman elites in the Senate and eventually led to his assassination. The beliefs that built the Republic had dissipated and the Empire phase was beginning.**

During the 1st century CE, the Empire experienced a period with few conflicts, known as Pax Romana or the Roman peace. Various emperors engaged in monumental building projects as they ended Rome's conquests. In the process, Rome began to lose its colonial economic base. Among the influences that would set the stage for reshaping Italian beliefs over the next few centuries were class struggle, failing trade, bureaucratic abuses, over-taxation, depletion of mineral resources, deforestation, soil erosion, balance of trade problems, currency devaluation, and the unavailability of capital due to confiscatory taxes. The most damaging change was the gradual loss of allegiance to what had become an imperial government. Romans saw their new government as less responsive to and less representative of those who fought to preserve and protect it.

By the 2nd century CE, Italy—the name of which is said to derive from an ancient king, Italus—had a population of about six million people. That represented less than ten percent of the Empire. Its centuries as a colonial economy made it expert at taking and distributing wealth but left it with little industry. It could no longer support a population dependent on its dwindling colonies. Its middle class suffered from economic decline and from increasing taxes. Roads and other infrastructure fell into disrepair. Government corruption and bureaucracy increased, and its reason for being increasingly became to collect taxes to support and perpetuate those in power. Many of the wealthy lived in villas, avoiding the crime and strife in the city. Some left the Empire altogether to preserve their assets. Available labor diminished as family size decreased and owning slaves became uneconomic.

Farmers in Italy and the colonies were caught between raiding barbarians and the government's tax collectors. As they conveyed their farms to landlords in exchange for protection and a share of the farm's production, they were sowing the seeds of feudalism. While students in the Roman Empire were learning literature, early science, and philosophy that reflected the influence of Greek beliefs on early Roman beliefs, their Greco-Roman belief system was about to undergo new psychogenetic evolutionary forces.

Rome acquires
early Christian psychogenes

By the time the Christian Church began to establish itself in the 2nd century, the Roman Empire, which had divided into Eastern and Western Empires, had already been weakened. Population decline in the Western Empire necessitated the importation of large numbers of Germanics. There wasn't enough time for them to assimilate Greco–Roman psychogenes. Imported Orientals (Middle Eastern peoples), on the other hand, didn't acquire Greco–Roman psychogenes because they wanted to destroy Roman culture. Germanic and Oriental populations increased within the Empire as Italian and Romanized cultures experienced declining populations. Simply by the size of their populations, Germanic and Oriental psychogenes were sufficient to dilute and weaken the then-existing Greco–Roman culture.

The effect of increasing despotism and declining religious fervor significantly undermined Roman beliefs that supported patriotism. The conquest of Greece had marked the beginning of religious decline as the old gods became less and less relevant. With patriotism and religion so intertwined, patriotism declined along with the old religious fervor. Now, the source of the Roman character and the stability of the Roman State began to evolve psychogenetically, with the assimilation of Christian psychogenes shaped by Church leaders whose apparent intent was to deny the military potential of Christians to the Roman

State. Salvian, a priest of Marseilles in the 5th century CE, without acknowledging that Church leaders had prevented Christians from serving in the Roman military, said the following:

> The Roman world is degenerating physically, has lost all moral valor, and leaves its defense to mercenary foreigners. How should such cowards deserve to survive? The Roman Empire is either dead, or drawing its last breath, even at the height of its luxury and games. Moritur et ridet—it laughs and dies.[5]

The problem Christianity created for the Roman State derived from its being a new form of evangelizing religion. Unlike polytheistic religions, which were tolerant of other religions and of secularists, Christian leaders did not tolerate the worship of other gods.[6] And, when their power permitted, they imposed their beliefs on others, using force to "convert" and retain believers. It appears that Church leaders employed strategies similar to those employed by the Roman Senate. In one example, to acquire additional power, Church leaders contrived a document purporting that Constantine donated much of the Roman Empire to the Roman Catholic Church. The forgery is referred to as "The Donation of Constantine."

Before Christian mythological psychogenes became part of the Roman belief system, Romans saw the Christian Church as subversive. Roman emperors had always been treated with the respect accorded to deities. For a Roman patriot, burning incense before the emperor's statue was equivalent to an American pledging allegiance to the flag. It was a matter of God and country. Americans during World War II and

Romans in the 1st century would have found much in common in their fusions of religion and patriotism. General George Patton's request that his chaplain write a prayer for God to grant clear weather so he could kill the enemy would have made perfect sense to Patton's Roman counterparts. However, when the Empire was under attack, Church leaders denied to the Emperor the military service of their Christian followers, claiming that religion was not subordinate to the State and that treating the Emperor as a deity represented polytheism and idolatry. **Church leaders contended that God supported the Christian Church, not Caesar. By separating the Church and the State, Church leaders denied Caesar the power of myth as a governing tool and as a means to rally the population to defend the borders. Christian leaders kept the Church and the State apart until recombining them when Emperor Constantine embraced Christianity.**

The 3rd century CE was a time when the Roman State was becoming increasingly unstable. Powerlessness and fear experienced by the population created fertile ground for a new, fortifying mythology. By promising an eternal, idyllic life after death, Christianity overcame the fear of death and gave power to the powerless. At the same time, some Romans were acquiring Christian psychogenes, the average Roman perceived Christian disinterest in defending the borders as shirking civic duty, regarding it as unpatriotic and as posing a threat to the future of the Empire. In contrast to other mythologies of the day, Christianity was perceived by the common Roman as aloof and condescending. In time, dislike for Christians became common. Citizens encouraged the government to punish them for insulting the State and Roman gods. Although there was an orthodox State mythology, it generally tolerated other mythologies provided they paid at least token respect to orthodox gods and the Emperor. This was a common attitude among polytheistic cultures. Eventually, growing popular hostility toward Christians was joined by resentment in government for Christian policies of overt disrespect for the Emperor and the Roman State.

Hostility toward Christians began when they were perceived as subversives. The level of hostility varied over the years. It was stronger during the barbarian attacks. As religious fervor, patriotism, and fear of invasion increased, the general population was confronted with unpatriotic Christians who refused to show any respect for the Emperor. No mention is made of unpatriotic and subversive behavior encouraged by Church leaders in early historical accounts by Church historians. Actual historical records and archeological evidence indicate that, in the entire Empire, there were small numbers of anti-Roman Christians who were killed as unpatriotic subversives when the borders were under attack. One historian described this time as follows:

> The only God that the Romans long refused to tolerate was the monotheistic and evangelizing god of the Christians. The Roman Empire did not require the Christians to give up their beliefs and rituals, but it did expect them to pay respect to the empire's protector gods and to the divinity of the Emperor. This was seen as a declaration of political loyalty. When the Christians vehemently refused to do so and went on to reject all attempts at compromise, the Romans reacted by persecuting what they

understood to be a politically subversive faction. And even this was done half-heartedly. In the 300 years from the crucifixion of Christ to the conversion of Emperor Constantine, polytheistic Roman emperors initiated no more than four general persecutions of Christians. Local administrators and governors incited some anti-Christian violence of their own. Still, if we combine all the victims of all these persecutions, it turns out that in these three centuries, polytheistic Romans killed no more than a few thousand Christians.[7, 8]

It is interesting to note that, unlike Church leaders in Rome, leaders of the Eastern Orthodox Church had no such adversarial relationship with the Caesars of the Eastern Roman Empire.

Near the end of the 2nd century, realizing that the Empire could not protect itself from barbarian threats if Christians refused to fight for Rome, some apparently secular Romans attempted to use reasoned arguments to defeat Christian myths. Their attempts failed, and Christian ranks continued to grow. In 311 CE, Emperor Galerius (305–311 CE) promulgated an edict of toleration that recognized Christianity as a lawful religion.

As the Western Roman Empire became more unstable in the 3rd century, many found comfort in the fortifying myths of Christianity. It seems likely that conversions to Christianity were enhanced by triggering Roman genetic chaperones. Examples include triggering eternal existence biases by emphasizing the Neo-Platonist view that human souls could join with God in an idyllic life after death, and by

**triggering conspiracy theories with exaggerated
stories of Roman persecutions of Christians.
Additional triggers would be encouraging
groupthink, appealing to Romans with a
conservative thinking style by emphasizing
security, and the importance of religious
authority figures.**

With its population swelling, the Christian Church
built cathedrals as the status of Christians increased,
and the influence of Christian leaders grew. The
Christian prohibition against marrying non-Christians
was eased as Christianity was becoming the dominant
religion.

Emperor Constantine (c.285–337 CE), a statesman
first and a supplicant second, realized that Christian
beliefs were replacing Greco–Roman religious beliefs.
He saw that Christians were strong, brave, and united
by strong beliefs, while the non-Christian population
no longer had the zeal and discipline that derived from
the beliefs of early Roman culture.

In 312 CE, Constantine prepared to battle
Maxentius for control of the Western Roman Empire.
From his youth to this time in his life, Constantine had
worshipped the Roman sun god Sol, as had his father.[9]
The day before battle, he claimed to have seen a
flaming cross in the sky with the inscription "in this
sign conquer."[10] On the day of battle he claimed to have
dreamed that a voice commanded him to have his
army's shields marked with the Christian cross. His
partly Christian army carried their symbol into battle,
and Constantine defeated Maxentius in the battle of
the Milvian Bridge, nine miles from Rome. In so doing,
he became Emperor of the Western Roman Empire. By
defeating Licinius eleven years later, Constantine
became Emperor of both the Eastern and Western

Roman Empires. **Once again, and under a new mythology, Romans had acquired a belief system that united them in the service of the State, and in the service of Church leaders in the Western Roman Empire. It appears that this rise to power of Church leaders, at least in part, had been accomplished by withholding their cooperation from the State until they and their religion was accepted.** Soon after, Constantine moved the capital from Rome to what would become Constantinople on the Bosporus Strait, in what is now Turkey. It remained the Roman capital (Nova Roma) until the last Emperor, Constantine XI, died defending Constantinople against the Ottomans in 1453.

The Roman Christian Church rejects Greco–Roman psychogenes

When Constantine declared himself a Christian, Roman psychogenetic evolution was complete. In about 300 years, the Roman Church had grown from a minority religion to the orthodox religion of the Roman Empire. And given the importance of Christian soldiers to the strength of Constantine's military, there is reason to believe that, at the time of his conversion, Constantine was performing the act of a general and a statesman.[11] Constantine is quoted as saying, "It is Fortuna [not God] that makes a man emperor."[12] Before he declared himself a Christian, Constantine had appointed non-Christian scholars and philosophers to his court.[13] After declaring himself a Christian, he paid little attention to

Christian leaders and theological concerns unless they influenced matters of state. His relationship with the bishops of the Church was that of a statesman with his administrators.

In 330 CE, Constantine had a monument erected in the city center to commemorate the declaration of Nova Roma (Constantinople) as the new capital of the Roman Empire. The monument was 50 meters tall with a statue of Constantine as the figure of Apollo on top. The Column of Constantine was dedicated on May 11, 330, with both Christian and pre-Christian religious ceremonies. It appears that Constantine continued to worship Sol (Apollo), the God of his father, which would explain why he wasn't baptized a Christian until he was on his deathbed. Beliefs about Apollo, learned during Constantine's childhood period of suggestibility, were not so easily changed.

During his reign, his relationship with Church leaders was symbiotic. In acquiring the political influence of the Church, which now taught the divine right of kings to its flock, Constantine consolidated and expanded his power. By endorsing Constantine, church leaders inherited the ecclesiastical administrative structure and mystical ritual of the pre-Christian Roman State. Popes in Rome would use both to spread Christian psychogenes throughout the fading Western Empire as Rome became established as the center of Christian Europe. Unlike Roman polytheistic religions, the popes continued to repress competing mythologies and the teaching of early science, philosophy, and literature, which were the core psychogenetic heritage of Greco–Roman culture. As Church leaders continued the high-living aspects of pre-Christian Rome, a number of devout Christians initiated a monastic movement to bring the Church more in line with the teachings of Christ.

Romulus Augustus, the last Western Roman Emperor, was deposed in 476. For the next 900 years, Roman Christian psychogenes were spread throughout Western Europe as Church leaders thwarted attempts to preserve Greco–Roman cultural and scientific accomplishments. Notwithstanding the fall of the Western Roman Empire, Greco–Roman beliefs continued to be taught in the Eastern Roman Empire. In 1453 CE Constantinople fell to the Ottomans. While Constantinople was the richest city in Europe in 1200 CE, it had been seriously weakened when it was sacked during the Fourth Crusade by the Doge of Venice with the complicity of Church leaders in Rome. It appears that the Doge sought riches, and Church leaders in Rome began the Crusades to dominate the Greek Orthodox Church in Constantinople.

Prior to 1453, Aristotelian logic was being taught in the Eastern Roman Empire and, in the 12th century, during the Islamic occupation of Southern Spain, it was reintroduced to European scholars by the Arab scholar Averroes. Aristotle's analytical method caused European scholars to question Christianity's claim that religious faith is supported by reason. William of Ockham, Niccolò Machiavelli, and many others challenged Church doctrine and beliefs. By the early 1500s, Martin Luther, who admired Ockham's work, protested the Roman Catholic Church's sale of indulgences (payment of money to remove sins). **In 1543, Nicolaus Copernicus published his model of the solar system with the Earth orbiting the**

sun, increasing challenges to the dogma and authority of the Church in Rome. Italian political theorist Niccolò Machiavelli wrote the following prophecy, reminiscent of Salvian's prediction for the Romans of his day:

> Had the religion of Christianity been preserved according to the ordinances of the Founder, the state and commonwealth of Christendom would have been far more united and happy than they are. Nor can there be a greater proof of its decadence than the fact that the nearer people are to the Roman Church, the head of their religion, the less religious are they. And whoever examines the principles on which that religion is founded, and sees how widely different from those principles its present practice and application are, will judge that her ruin or chastisement is near at hand.[14]

The Church's version of events during this period in history was examined in 1950 by Joseph McCabe (1867–1955). He had been ordained a Catholic priest (Father Anthony) in 1890, but five years later, his lingering doubts about the Church's teachings caused him to leave the priesthood. Being an outstanding scholar, he wrote and lectured on religion and other subjects. He believed that the Columbia Encyclopedia was parroting Church historical propaganda and that it used the Catholic Encyclopedia instead of the work of historians as a source for articles.

In 1950, Joseph McCabe wrote *The Columbia Encyclopedia's Crimes Against the Truth,* which criticized the Columbia Encyclopedia for

misstating facts to favor the Church's self-serving version of history and its attempts to repress Greco-Roman culture and science. He said that during the Dark Ages, rather than preserving Greco-Roman culture, the Church ignored the fine results achieved in the science of Alexandria and the social-welfare programs of the Roman Empire. He claimed that the Encyclopedia failed to mention that the popes had foiled attempts to bring back both of those Greco–Roman accomplishments; instead of admitting that it brought darkness on civilization, the encyclopedia claimed that the Church brought light into a dark world and made heroic efforts to preserve the accomplishments of the Roman Empire. McCabe wrote that the Encyclopedia described the Crusades as an outcome of the highest point of religious devotion and were begun to protect Christians in the Holy Land. However, McCabe wrote, Pope Urban II's sermon calling for the First Crusade offered knights the prospect of riches, and experts on the Crusades acknowledge that the knights' predominant motives were greed, love of fighting, and liberation from their heavy feudal burdens at home. In addition, the basis for the Crusades was false because Turks in the holy land did not hinder Christians. **McCabe wrote further that the Church's real motivation was to expand its power by bringing the Greek Church under the control of the Church in Rome. Exactly that was admitted by Pope John Paul II in 2001.**[15,16] **It might be said that, rather than the Western Roman Empire falling, early Church leaders used their understanding of governance to evolve from a Roman political State into a Roman religious State, which today has a global**

income that ranks as the 53rd largest "economy" out of about 190 nations.

Greco–Roman psychogenes return with the Renaissance

In the 12th century, Southern Spain was occupied by Moors. At that time, the Moorish physician-philosopher Averroes was asked to write commentaries on Aristotle. Until that time, **Aristotle's logic in Europe had been relegated by Augustine and church scholars to searching for rational support for theological dogma. By reintroducing Aristotelian logic to Europe, Averroes' commentaries profoundly affected the thinking of theologians and scholars of the day by causing them to focus on the opposition between faith and reason.** By 1277, Aristotelian challenges to Church dogma caused the Bishop of Paris to issue a condemnation and to threaten the excommunication of those who taught "Averroism" or "radical Aristotelianism." **The Greco-Roman belief system that had evolved into Roman Christian beliefs was about to evolve once more. As the 14th century began, William of Ockham (1287–1347 CE) and philosopher Marsilius of Padua (c.1290–c.1343 CE) openly challenged church dogma with rediscovered Aristotelian logic. This was followed by an admirer of Ockham, Martin Luther (1483–1546 CE), who began the Protestant Reformation in 1517. By the middle of the 15th century, rediscovered Greco–Roman beliefs blossomed into the Italian Renaissance under** the **Medici in Florence**. Life was once again seen as an opportunity and not merely a veil of tears. **During the 16ᵗʰ century, the evolving Italian Renaissance rediscovered Greco–Roman philosophy, art, science, architecture, and literature, and returned secular (non-religious) learning to Europe. Intellectual freedom reappeared after languishing for almost a thousand years. Thanks to the preservation of Greco–Roman learning in the Eastern Roman Empire and to ongoing scholarly efforts such as the recent discovery of the Antikythera astronomical analog computer, and a prayer book that wrote over Archimedes' mathematical notes on an early version of calculus, Italians began to resurrect the accomplishments of their Greco-Roman ancestors.**

Philosophers who shaped Western psychogenetic evolution

In the 5ᵗʰ century BCE, Plato traveled and studied with philosophers in Greece and priests in Egypt. He believed in a theoretical level of perfection of things and ideas, which he believed could not be achieved. In addition, he believed that a God was the first cause that set the universe in motion. However, **his view was that God did not intervene in human affairs. His views appear to be consistent with a strong eternal existence bias supported by a disregard for evidence, which is described as his distrust of the senses.**

He sought to teach ethics to Athenians without relying on myth or superstition. In time, he realized that the mass of society is more easily controlled by myth-driven constraints than by reason. **The contrast between his perfect ideas and imperfect fellow humans resulted in his viewing humans as having a divine spirit, but an evil nature. This aspect of Plato's philosophy, although unappealing to his Greek contemporaries, would appeal to early Christians. Was Plato disappointed by his fellow Greeks, whose perceptions were dominated by their genetic chaperones?** Subsequently, **Plotinus (c.204/5–270) transformed Platonism into Neo-Platonism by adding the mystical concept of individual souls joining with God. Via Neo-Platonism, Plato influenced Christianity.**

Aristotle studied with Plato in Athens. While Plato imagined the world to be an imperfect reflection of perfect forms and ideas, **Aristotle relied on observations provided by his senses and applied deductive reasoning to unravel the secrets of Nature. It appears that he was beginning to use logic and evidence to refine genetic chaperone-created perceptions of reality.** Unlike Plato, whose thinking lacked the reasoned structure needed to unravel Nature's secrets, Aristotle was beginning to invent a systematic method to do just that. **Much as the ancient philosophers extracted philosophy from a quagmire of animism, myth, and illusory perceptions, Aristotle managed to extract an early version of the scientific method from Ancient Greek speculations about Nature.** For

2,000 years, his treatises were the textbook of logic for the Western world. **His influence was such that, had he accepted the view of other Greek philosophers that biological evolution progressed by natural selection, Darwinism by another name would probably have predated Christianity by centuries.**

In the 4th century, CE Augustine was a church father and philosopher. For a time, his skepticism about the nature of reality left him with unanswered questions that were emotionally unfulfilling. He studied Platonism and Neo-Platonism. However, **it was the Bible, and particularly the symbolic interpretation of biblical accounts by Paul of Tarsus, that appealed to Augustine.** He related to Paul's doubts and found comfort in blind faith that skepticism could not provide. **For Augustine, blind faith (belief without evidence) afforded him mental peace. Did Augustine ultimately reject Aristotle's test of logic and evidence and accept as valid the emotionally fulfilling perceptions of his genetic chaperone?** When Augustine became a Christian, he brought with him Neo-Platonism. His logic, when applied to religion, made him exceptional among Church philosophers. **For the new church, his 230 treatises were foundation stones that incorporated Neo-Platonism (the rejection of evidence and an acceptance that human souls could join with God) into Christian thinking.** Although his passion and intellect influenced the thinking and history of Western Christianity, Eastern (Greek Orthodox) Christianity did not care for his anti-intellectual valuing of emotion over reason. **Among Augustine's beliefs were that God's existence could be verified using logic and that** the Church should *dominate both government and thought*, which Roman Catholicism had done until the Renaissance. After Augustine, Christian scholars sought to use Aristotle's method of analysis for the limited purpose of supporting Church mythological beliefs (confirmatory bias?).

Islamist philosophers (falsafi) became aware of Aristotle from their dealings with the Eastern Roman Empire. **The 12th-century Islamic philosopher Averroes reintroduced Aristotelian logic to European scholars in commentaries he wrote to explain Aristotelian thinking. In so doing, he reintroduced Europe to Aristotle's Greco-Roman analytical method, which caused European scholars to question Christianity's claim that religious faith is supported by reason.**

William of Ockham, a Franciscan monk, considered to be among the most brilliant thinkers of the 14th century, used reintroduced Aristotelian logic to question the Church's forced marriage of reason and religion. Ockham used his analytical "razor", which contends that among competing theories, the simplest theory that relies on what is already known is more likely to be true. He used his "razor" to dissect the Church's dogma that layered unprovable supposition upon unprovable supposition. He questioned the apostolic succession of the popes and papal infallibility. **The opposition of Ockham and others to Augustine's contention that reason can prove the truth of the tenets of religion was widely accepted. In time, that acceptance resulted in a slow psychogenetic evolution away from the treatises of Augustine.** Although the Church resisted change, it could not stop its psychogenetic evolution. In time, Martin Luther declared Ockham to be the most ingenious of scholastic doctors. **From Aristotle to Ockham to Luther, the seeds of the Reformation had been sown.**

In the 16th century, Giordano Bruno attended a Dominican monastery where Thomas Aquinas had taught. Soon his **unorthodox views caused him to leave both the monastery and Italy.** He moved to Paris, where he quickly became known to Henry III. Among his numerous books was one that refuted contentions that the dogmas of the Church could be proven by reason. Bruno contended that Christianity is irrational and that it is accepted through blind faith, and that revelation has no scientific basis. **While visiting England, Bruno's support of the view that the Earth orbited the sun fell on unbelieving ears—it was contrary to Aristotle's view.** At that time, Galileo had not yet endorsed Copernicus' view that the Earth orbited the sun, in contradiction of Church dogma.

Some of Bruno's writings dealt with superstition and the narrow and tiresome focus of Catholic and Protestant teachings on trivialities—concepts that would be taken up by Descartes, who would be born a few years later. He believed that the Church encouraged ignorance. One of Bruno's heresies was that he believed that God and Nature could not be separated. It was considered heretical because it attributed to God the physical limits of Nature.

When he returned to Italy, he was delivered into the hands of the Inquisition. His heresy was in believing that one's soul could join with God through wisdom. On February 9, 1600, he was sentenced to death at the palace of the Grand Inquisitor. When he heard his sentence, Bruno said, "Perhaps you, my judges, pronounce this sentence against me with greater fear than I receive it." Refusing to repent, eight days later, he was burned alive, scornfully pushing away a crucifix offered to him as the flames ended his life.

Bruno's philosophical views became an intimate part of the Dutch philosopher Baruch Spinoza's (1632–1677) thinking,[12] and anticipated theories of the German philosopher Gottfried Leibniz (1646–1716). **Bruno represented a transition to modern philosophy. His radical view of how the universe worked contradicted Aristotle's view of the universe and the Church's view of God and a perfect firmament. Bruno has been recognized as a martyred philosopher in the intellectual renaissance that ended the Church's anti-Greco–Roman, anti-intellectual hold on European thinking begun by Augustine in the 5th century.** It might be said that the Italian Renaissance, which began in the 14th century with the rebirth of Greco–Roman culture, was completed when Giordano Bruno championed the rebirth of freethought, science, and philosophy. Although the Renaissance marked the beginning of a new era for Europe, it took hold unevenly. **With the burning of Bruno and the house arrest of Galileo, the center of European philosophy and science moved north to Protestant Europe.**

The philosophers who most influenced 2,000 years of Italian history might be said to fall into two groups—poets and scientists—with the perceptions of poets relying more on their genetic chaperones and those of the scientists

relying more on analytical thinking. Perhaps Plato inherited a strong intentionality bias that shaped his perception of an apparently planned universe that he believed was begun by a deity's first cause. Augustine, in turn, unsatisfied with questions rational analysis could not answer, perhaps preferred to believe myths that satisfied his intuitions, thinking style, and other aspects of the genetic chaperone he inherited. Alternatively, perhaps inheriting a liberal thinking style produced the rational analysis of Ockham and Bruno that challenged the dogma of Augustine's mythology. To what extent were these philosophers puppets dancing on evolution's stage to the tune of their genetic chaperone's versions of reality?

Chapter 6

Vulnerabilities of our belief systems and genetic chaperones

When our ancestors were painting animal scenes on cave walls, their genetic chaperones aided their survival by causing them to perceive fictitious versions of reality. While giving them a sense of personal control,[1] those fictitious perceptions were also shaping their belief systems.

Genetic chaperones and beliefs

It seems apparent that our DNA provides us with mental biases, traits, and neurochemicals that differ in strength from person to person. To aid our survival, they alter our perceptions in a way that can incline us to believe that magical thinking is real. Researchers have observed that our mythological perspectives derive from a "basic impulse" of the human mind.[2,3] By combining this with other research, we might reasonably conclude that this human impulse (a religious, spiritual, or awe-inspired response to events) derives from brain traits, biases, and neurochemicals that "incline us to believe" in a mythical or magical world.[4] For example, the eternal existence bias appears to predispose us to perceive that an aspect of our minds exists separate from our bodies and that a part of us exists before and after our physical existence. It predisposes us to perceive a reality in which a non-physical part of us (a personal spirit) survives our death within a culture-specific narrative. **To the extent that this happens, the same biases and traits that aid our survival contribute to our perceiving reality from a mythological perspective.**

Do illusory correlations contribute to a mythological perspective? A fourteen-year study published by the American Psychological Association's *Health Psychology Journal*[5] examined people's perceived ability to exert influence over life circumstances. While less educated people are more likely to experience disease, disability, and premature death, research shows that less educated **people with a strong sense of control over events have significantly increased life expectancies. If praying increases someone's sense of control over events, they are more likely to live longer. While they are likely to believe that their prayers were answered, this research shows that it is actually their increased sense of control that increases their life expectancy.**

Other research shows that having religious or spiritual perceptions can create positive feelings in the brain's pleasure center, similar to the positive feelings experienced with love, sex, gambling, drugs, and music. **When this happens, devoutly religious people are likely to believe**

that feeling good is confirmation that their religious beliefs are true.[6]

While religions have an altruistic aspect, there are religions with all-knowing, moralistic, punitive gods that promote cooperation among their believers by employing a supernatural admonition equivalent to "I know what you are doing. I command you to cooperate with fellow believers and if you don't treat your fellow believers fairly I will punish you."[7] That threat of divine retribution is a believable inducement to cooperate for those whose genetic chaperones predispose them to believe in the supernatural and an afterlife. The resulting cooperation will have survival value, and believers' supportive biases and traits will be passed to the next generation.

When, in the not too distant past, our genetic chaperones acquired an intentionality bias, our ancestors were able to speculate about what others were thinking. Today, this bias causes us to assume that things we observe were intended by someone, i.e., that they were planned.[8] For the first time in human history, this bias enabled our ancestors to question why things are the way they are. Being able to ask this question would have contributed to ancestral mythological speculations about supernatural intentions. In particular, they would have speculated about who or what intended the world to be the way it is. The intentionality bias appears to underlie the argument Darwin faced, i.e., if something as complex as a watch has a watchmaker, then something as complex as the universe must have a creator.

Can a conservative or liberal thinking style favor a mythological world view? According to a study in 2012, believing in a god correlates with having inherited a conservative thinking style[9] (not political preference). That thinking style causes us to be comfortable with certainty, structure, and predictability; resistant to change in established modes of behavior; and supportive of leaders we think will enhance our security. These same characteristics are common to religious organizations that provide certainty, structure, predictability, and resistance to change, and decisive religious leaders who personify security. **Inasmuch as the basic elements of a religious perspective correspond to conservative thinking style characteristics, simply inheriting a conservative thinking style appears to predispose us to religiosity. Other factors might involve inheriting a strong eternal existence bias and myth-supportive brain traits such as being insensitive to intuitive/reflective memory conflicts that cause us to rely more on intuitive memories and less on analytical thinking.**

Similarly, we might be predisposed to think about problems by defaulting to our intuitive thinking region instead of our analytical thinking region. When this happens, by beginning to think intuitively about mythological matters, we are prevented from thinking about them analytically. **Defaulting to our intuitive thinking region might also reinforce intuitive thoughts about our illusory correlations, dreams, and magical thinking.**

In summary, the spiritual "impulse" or sense of religiosity that many of us experience might result from inheriting a strong eternal existence bias, a conservative thinking style, a

strong confirmation bias, assuming that things that just happened were planned, defaulting to our intuitive thinking region, and being raised with a belief system that confirms the magical thinking perceptions of our genetic chaperones.

Our two-thinking style advantage

It appears that inheriting genetic chaperones with characteristics of various intensities, together with belief systems that bias our perceptions with apperception and the like, cause the way we think to fall somewhere between mostly conservative and mostly liberal. Within that spectrum, we tend to favor those with views similar to our own. When we form groups based on our similarities, the influence of our world view is amplified and might be sufficient to influence our group's social evolution. We saw this take place in the Roman Empire when Roman Christians became numerous enough to suppress competing religions, consistent with Augustine's caveat to dominate both government and thought—what I call a winners-take-all bias. From the winner's point of view, it would be difficult to consider making decisions that reflect beliefs very different from their own. This winners-take-all bias likely contributed to the Dark Ages as it used dogma, the banning of books, and the Inquisitions to repress the thinking of countless people in most of Europe for most of a millennium. By requiring that solutions to problems be consistent with their conservative or liberal world view, winners-take-all groups sow the seeds of future problems by not considering the perspectives and solutions of the non-winners.

Have you wondered why we have two primary thinking styles and not just one? Did two thinking styles evolve, perhaps resulting from different gephyrin levels, because together they represent a survival advantage for social groups? Are these thinking styles complementary sides of the same ancient coin? With their different perceptions of reality and solutions to problems, it appears that the larger array of perspectives and solutions provided by combining these thinking styles gives us a survival advantage over each thinking style alone. It is analogous to focusing on an object first with both eyes open and then with either the left or right eye closed. Clearly, there is a focusing advantage to having both eyes open. While there are other hypotheses, it is possible that a two-thinking style advantage would have evolved without difficulty in small social groups of perhaps up to 150 people in size.[10] At that size, we tend to know personally everyone in the group, including those with whom we disagree and why they think as they do. Larger groups, however, make it possible to know mainly those who have our thinking style. In essence, large groups make thinking style factions possible, with each faction having a winners-take-all bias. These faction bubbles make it possible to ignore half of what was our Stone Age two-thinking style advantage. Such bubbles make possible winners-take-all dominance that can create extended periods of extreme liberal or conservative thinking style decision-making. Over time, that domination would weaken large social groups as stabilizing actions consistent with the beliefs and perspectives of the non-winners are ignored. **The irony is that the two-thinking style advantage that benefited small Stone Age social groups can produce socially destructive results in the large and complex social groups of today.**

To avoid extremes, the Ancient Greeks sought to find a harmonious middle path. Their concept, called the Golden Mean, might well be applied today to deal with the winners-take-all bias we see around us. Today, the Golden Mean would encourage us to avoid electing, supporting, or endorsing those whose genetic-chaperone-dominated thinking is on the extremes of the conservative/liberal spectrum. In so doing, those who come to power would have less extreme views and would be more likely to consider the perspectives and opinions of their opposition. By negotiating, their combined options would not be limited by winners-take-all thinking and would avoid legislative gridlock.

Research shows that politicians with extreme conservative or liberal views feel superior regarding their beliefs and are inclined to arrogantly assert their opinions as fact.[11] Why does this happen? If we acquire beliefs that are compatible with our thinking style and other biases and traits, those of us with a liberal thinking style are likely to acquire beliefs that involve ambiguity, curiosity, and novelty, but not things involving societal constraints. And, alternatively, those of us with a conservative thinking style are likely to acquire beliefs that involve structure and predictability, but not beliefs that require a change in the way we normally do things.

If we inherit a fundamentalist belief system and a conservative thinking style, we would

probably think that our way of seeing the world is not biased. We might sincerely perceive contradictions to our beliefs or perceptions as incomprehensible. Consequently, we might respond to contradiction with a sense of superiority and perhaps arrogance that might derive from indignation. By comparison, those with less-intense, non-extreme views are less likely to be motivated by emotion and to participate in making group decisions by voting. This lack of participation by the "unmotivated center" gives power to winners-take-all extremists and might explain, in part, why extreme political and religious organizations have dominated much of our history.

Once in power, people with a strong belief superiority bias have no tolerance for competing ideas. This appears to be a key motivation for proselytizing religions and extreme political movements. Such people are blind to their biases and compound the problem by accepting only like-minded people into their groups. In time, they might change the beliefs of others under their control through fear, intimidation, propaganda, biasing the law, indoctrinating the young, and the like. In part, they make their worldview dominant by engaging in propaganda and psychogenetic manipulation.

Bias blindness

For our genetic chaperones to be effective, we are born blind to their existence. We are born unaware of our negativity bias, conservative or liberal thinking style, illusory correlations, focusing illusions, belief system apperceptions, and other biases and traits. From our point of view, we think we see reality as it is. It's analogous to colorblindness. However, unlike dealing with colorblindness by accepting that we are born blind to certain colors, bias blindness is less detectable and more disturbing. Unlike simply accepting that we are colorblind, with bias blindness, we need to accept that reality might be different from what we perceive it to be.

It is likely that our ability to acknowledge that we have bias blindness varies from person to person. For those who inherit strong biases, certain brain traits, and fundamentalist beliefs, it would be difficult to believe that they are blind to the perception distortions of their genetic chaperones. For this reason, depending on the subject, discussing reality with someone who has strong bias blindness might be equivalent to discussing impressionist paintings with someone who is colorblind. Even those with less-strong bias blindness might be unwilling to acknowledge that they misperceive reality if doing so would disrupt their economic or political power or the family and community relationships that are the fabric of their lives.

Bias blindness kept our Stone Age ancestors alive when they were hunted by predators and when they understood very little about reality as it is. As our ancestors became more social and their ability to reason improved, their bias blindness contributed to shaping the more complex belief systems they formed. Little changed until ancestors, such as the Ancient Greeks, began to examine reality in a reasoned

and systematic way. Their more analytical view of reality represented an alternative to our reliance on genetically chaperoned thinking that underlies animism, magical thinking, superstition, sorcery, conspiracy theories, and the like. Their reasoned and systematic way of thinking represented an alternative to their history of shameful acts caused by ancestral decisions based not on reality, but on the chaperone-altered versions of reality to which our ancestors were blind. The question today is, will the genetic chaperones that enabled our Stone Age ancestors to get through their day with stone-tipped spears be helpful or harmful in today's world, where spears are thrown in the form of rockets and are tipped with nuclear weapons?

Perhaps a takeaway of this book is that we have difficulty agreeing on what reality is because our beliefs about what is true derive from a number of perception-distorting influences—one being the way brain traits such as apperception, dysrationalia, and the Semmelweis reflex limit our ability to acquire new beliefs or to change existing beliefs. Another reason being that our belief systems accumulate organized ignorance. Today, we see the process of genetic chaperones shaping belief systems in the conflicting perceptions that underlie culture wars, climate change denial, childhood vaccinations, genetically modified foods, multiculturalism, and fake news.[12] It appears that evidence-based reasoning is being replaced with anti-enlightenment attitudes that derive from undisclosed fears, ideologies, worldviews, identity needs, and hidden anti-enlightenment activities of vested interests in business, politics, and religion.[13] In addition, it has been shown that we might cling to unrealistic beliefs if our most recent expressions of those beliefs are confirmed by others. Interactions with like-minded people and engaging in social-media bubble realities can both provide such confirmation.[14]

In recent history, we have seen oil and tobacco interests invest heavily in promoting junk science or in falsely accusing others of using junk science to create doubt in the minds of the public and to preserve their profits. Politicians are doing the same for political gain. In so doing, they damage the believability of science in the minds of the public. **History shows that the scientific method of analysis has proven to be effective in sorting through conjecture and speculation to discover what reality is. However, if the public has been conditioned to distrust our best understanding of what reality is, then what understanding of reality will guide us in making decisions that avoid disappointment or disaster?**

For the most part, those of us who make things happen in the tangible world rely on verifiable evidence and a disciplined method of reasoning to determine which beliefs about reality are true. That is why our smartphones work. However, beliefs about intangible matters, by definition, are not verifiable with tangible evidence. **To determine which of our intangible beliefs are true, many rely on intuitions and on faith or a motivation to believe something without evidence. To the extent that intangible beliefs derive from** incorrect inherited beliefs about reality or from genetic-chaperone-altered perceptions, at best, intangible beliefs only partially reflect reality as it is.

Hacking our genetic chaperones

Long before recorded history, Nature evolved our ancestors' biases and brain traits in a way that chaperoned their behaviors to help them survive. Today, triggering our genetic chaperones causes us to respond non-consciously in ways that were appropriate for our ancestors' survival. If we do not rely on evidence and disciplined thinking but relate to the world primarily by relying on the responses of our genetic chaperones, we expose ourselves to being manipulated by people who understand how our biases and brain traits work. Propagandists know how to create artificial conditions calculated to trigger Stone Age biases that cause us to think that the "fake reality" they create is real. Politicians, religions, businesses, individuals, and various organizations employ propagandists to achieve their goals by using ego, fear, and other bias triggers to create fake realities that achieve their goals. When they succeed, we behave much like string puppets. For example, propagandists know that our genetic chaperones are likely to respond with fear and suspicion if we are exposed to social media stories that trigger our prejudices or threaten the welfare of our ethnic, social, religious, economic, or other groups. When we become fearful, it is difficult for us to switch from emotional (intuitive) thinking to thinking rationally and to question the truth of what we are being told. Propagandists trigger ego, herd behavior, and other biases when they stage large, impressive events to exaggerate their economic or other accomplishments and to convey a sense of community and unity within the context of the propagandists' version of reality. During such events, flattering posters and videos might be used that show us participating in the propagandists' fake reality. In this case, our genetic chaperones incline us to herd behavior or groupthink and thereby, to endorse the group's "trusted leader."

To protect their fake reality, propagandists attempt to convince us not to believe people and organizations that are in a position to reveal the truth about what the propagandists are doing. To accomplish this, propagandists use emotionally stimulating lies, personal attacks, defamatory names, slogans, images, partial truths, and arguments that use deceptive logical fallacies to cause us not to believe journalists, established institutions, respected individuals, and intelligence-gathering organizations that are a threat to the propagandists' fake reality. The goal of these strategies is to create a fake reality that convinces us to weaken competitors of the propagandists' client and, in politics, to give their client political power. In politics, clients of propagandists can use the power we give them to convince governmental institutions to do their bidding. As history shows, some use the power we give them to remove impediments to their acquiring control of the government. If the propagandists are foreign governments, their goal is more likely to cause distrust and dissension to bias elections or to otherwise interfere with our democratic, economic or other processes. It appears that the increasing separation of liberal and conservative political positions in democratic countries, for the most part, is attributable to both the closing of minds that consume only "news" that confirms existing beliefs, and to the efforts of propagandists that use things such as voter suppression and *them* vs. *us* manipulation to pit us against each other to disrupt our democratic processes.

For propagandists to succeed in using our genetic chaperones against us, they must prevent us from discovering what they are doing. Given that our perceptions derive from a need to survive and not from a need to see reality as it is, to perceive reality clearly through the fog of our biases, we need to be aware that our genetic chaperones are shaping our perceptions. When we permit our confirmation bias to seek news only from sources we agree with, and when we permit groupthink and a desire to agree with and feel part of the herd to influence our thinking, we are allowing our genetic chaperones to prevent us from seeing reality as it is. In a 24/7 news environment, should we allow our genetic chaperone's focusing illusion to exaggerate the importance of issues to which we are constantly exposed? Should we learn about logical fallacies to avoid being tricked with rhetoric into believing in fake realities? Perhaps learning to recognize when propagandists are triggering our genetic chaperones would be the most effective way to avoid being manipulated. One strategy to induce us to support their agenda involves propagandists triggering our genetic chaperones to support a *them* vs. *us* fake reality where the propagandists' political opposition and other out-groups are *them*. To do this, they create oversimplified, negative images of *them* (clustering illusion, logical fallacies, negativity bias) and ego-enhancing images of *us* (superiority bias, self-serving bias). In addition, we are told that what *we* do is good and successful, and what *they* do is inferior, unproductive, and dangerous. Portraying *them* as unattractive, untrustworthy, or otherwise (negativity bias, ascription bias—where the personalities, moods, and behaviors of *us* are seen as flexible, and those of *them* are seen as rigid) further separates *them* from *us*. This strategy converts *us* into an in-group with common enemies that we are ready to make decisions against.

As more of us accept the propagandist's fake separation of *them* vs. *us*, the in-group grows, and others are likely to join in (bandwagon effect). When the *them* vs. *us* mindset becomes established, contradictory evidence is ignored (Semmelweis reflex, i.e., rejecting evidence that conflicts with existing beliefs). By portraying *us* as hard-working, moral, and fair, we treat each other preferentially (in-group bias), which further separates *us* from *them*. Once enough of us accept propagandists' *them* vs. *us* manipulations, those who don't buy into herd instinct, in-group bias, and bandwagon effect thinking are nonetheless likely to consider mimicking or adopting in-group behaviors to avoid ostracism or worse. As the *us* group becomes dominant, it can be manipulated to become desensitized to immoral or unlawful behaviors against *them*. We saw this happen to the Jews and others in Nazi Germany, and to a lesser extent we see it happening in countries where immigrants are being defined as *them* for political reasons. To enforce their agenda, propagandists invoke the superiority bias, self-serving bias, and bandwagon effect to induce us to patriotism in the military service of their clients' goals. This aspect of Nazi propaganda in World War II resulted in more than 60 million people being killed.

Biases used by propagandists to deify a leader include the halo effect and authority bias, which might cause us to think that a tall and handsome leader in a military uniform is also brave and smart and that his opinions are accurate and deserving of respect. When surrounded by a majority that approves of the leader, our herd instinct will cause us to feel safer if we follow the herd. It is similar to wanting to hop on the bandwagon. The leader will stage large events with an *us* vs. *them* speech presented as good vs. evil. The leader's speech will trigger the biases of an eager audience whose receptive minds have been carefully manipulated by propagandists. **Evolution provided us with genetic chaperones to deal with Stone Age predators. It did not provide us with a similar genetic process to deal with modern humans who use our genetic chaperones to manipulate our perceptions and behaviors.**

The internet has increased the reach of propagandists. When the internet became available to the public in the 1990s, many thought it was the beginning of a beneficial era of connectedness. However, by the beginning of the 21st century, a pivotal change had taken place that was unique in human history. It happened when **computer technology companies combined neuroscience, psychology, and computing technology. More** specifically, by triggering the in-group bias of users' genetic chaperones with software that incorporated "friends lists", computer technology companies were able to keep computer users connected longer to game and social media websites. By using "addictive" websites, longer connection time exposed users to more advertising and enabled these data collection companies to accumulate more user behavior data, both of which increased data collection company profits. And, with no governmental regulation, these companies developed more sophisticated graphic and other manipulative data collection methods with no concern for user privacy. Data such as user "likes", inquiries, purchase choices, friends, and user moral outrage responses to culture wars and election-related fake news enabled these data collection companies to accumulate more detailed user psychological and other profiles. In addition to being used internally, those profiles were sold to other companies to further the data company's business.[15] **Politicians quickly realized that having access to individual voter profiles enabled them to influence elections, not with traditional mass propaganda methods, but with individually targeted personalized propaganda.** Voter suppression was at the top of their list. Politicians and others began manipulating elections with data company profiles that revealed users' genetic chaperones. With access to vast databases of behavioral information and with the cost of distributing propaganda being insignificant, political propagandists began sending messages, tweets, and fake news to millions of voters. In addition, part of the public they are now able to access and manipulate is the previously difficult-to-reach segment that does not rely on books and print media for their information but does use social media. **Personalized propaganda took cognitive hacking to a new level. This new and ominous era of personalized propaganda was just one effect of growing surveillance capitalism.** Instead of realizing early optimistic predictions that the internet would enable users to reach out to the world, data collection companies, and data processing methods such as artificial intelligence, have enabled commercial and political interests to manipulate many users as if they were string puppets. By analogy, when Romans built roads across their increasing territory, they did not foresee that those roads would help vandals to invade their homeland.

We know that manipulating our biases is not new. **For millennia, political regimes and religions have triggered the biases of their subjects variously with emotionally stimulating architecture, paintings, sculptures, music, singing, symbols of power, and the like. These relatively unsophisticated efforts to manipulate our biases and brain traits pale when compared with what propagandists can do today by hacking our genetic chaperones. Given that we are born blind to our biases, our psychological profiles enable hackers to manipulate our behavior with more understanding than we have of ourselves.**

It appears that propagandists around the world are using people's psychological profiles to trigger genetic chaperone responses to promote anti-democratic changes in democratic

countries. **News media and judicial systems are being weakened by propagandists to strengthen authoritarian governments. If successful, hacking our genetic chaperones can turn the concept of democratic free choice into an illusion.**

In response to these developments, the European Union has taken action to protect E.U. members' personal information with The General Data Protection Regulation (EU) 2016/679 ("GDPR"). Given the global nature of data collection companies, E.U. regulations will likely benefit everyone and provide a basis for legislation in other countries. Perhaps, in the near future, the entrepreneurial energy that inadvertently benefited propagandists will provide a new generation of software that will reveal when genetic chaperone triggers are being used and how to identify fake news. The quality of fake news generated by artificial intelligence is now so convincing that, for many people, it might take artificial intelligence to detect it. In the meantime, learning to recognize how our genetic chaperones can be triggered should help to protect against propaganda being used to manipulate and divide us.

Competing realities

We began our journey with the question:

If there is only one reality, why can't we agree on what it is?

We soon became aware that the brain we inherited has the same survival characteristics as that of our Stone Age ancestors. Their mental biases and traits enabled them to survive, not because they understood their world, but because their biases and traits provided them with an approximated or simulated understanding of reality. By exaggerating their fears and self-images with fictitious perceptions, their mental biases and traits provided them with the caution and self-confidence they needed to survive. While being chaperoned in this way, our ancestors were unaware that the belief systems they were forming reflected their genetic chaperones' fictitious versions of reality. As their world increased in complexity, they perceived intent and correlations where none existed. Their genetic chaperones' fictitious perceptions caused them to believe that animism was real. Belief systems that passed from generation to generation were filled with erroneous beliefs about the nature of reality. However, about three thousand years ago, a small number of people in various places around the world began to question their beliefs and perceptions of reality. They were becoming aware that the reality they perceived was not necessarily reality as it is. Over the centuries since then, that awareness matured into a method of evidence-based rational analysis that significantly improved our ability to know whether our perceptions of reality are valid.

Our history has left us with competing realities. The first exists because our genetic chaperones cause us to believe that our survival-based, fictional versions of reality are real. **The second was formed when we began to manage our genetic chaperones by verifying our perceptions with logic, reasoning, and evidence.** In view of the global problems we face today, which of our competing realities should we rely on to deal with global problems such as religious wars, the collapse of fisheries, the decreasing availability of freshwater, and so on?

We acquired our genetic chaperones by a repetitive trial and error selection process that gradually adapted our mental biases and traits to enhance our survival. Without experiencing repeated trial and error survival events, mental biases, and traits cannot form. For this reason, we have no mental biases or traits to deal with seldom repeating events such as a gradually rising sea level and a global drop in freshwater supplies. Unlike hearing a noise in the dark that makes us fearful, our genetic chaperones do not respond when we observe steadily increasing flooding in cities around the world. For this reason, expecting our genetic chaperones to respond to threats they never experienced would be foolish. An analogy would be to instinctively grasp the mooring line of a rising, out of control hot air balloon. Letting go as you leave the ground will save your life while holding on as long as you can will cause you to fall from a life-threatening height. In this analogy, using reason to override your genetic chaperone's response to hold on would likely save your life. Similarly, by managing our genetic chaperones' responses, we can address problems with the kind of understanding that put humans on the moon, cures disease, and has produced achievements that virtually define the modern world. **It seems clear that viewing reality with well-reasoned understanding and not the simulated understanding of our genetic chaperones is more likely to be successful in dealing with the problems we face today.**

In addition to conflicts between chaperone-based and reason-based thinking, chaperone-based groups often create belief systems that conflict with each other because they derive from arbitrary national, religious, ethnic, and other beliefs. By comparison, learning to understand and manage the fictions of their genetic chaperones enables engineers and scientists from around the world to create and refine substantially identical and verifiable belief systems.

In large part, our genetic chaperones underlie our sordid and callous history of social conflict. The same Stone Age mental biases and traits our ancestors relied on to survive have shaped much of modern thinking. For this reason, it appears that our conflicts, for the most part, are not the result of insincere or immoral motivations. They more likely result from people being indoctrinated instead of being educated to think both analytically and with the self-discipline needed to accept disappointing evidence. Instead, we are all trying to deal with the world in which we find ourselves with the beliefs we inherited, and with the genetic chaperones Nature gave us.

If the strife created by our genetic chaperones is dismaying and the thought of managing our genetic chaperones is daunting or unsettling, consider this: just knowing how

our chaperone shapes the way we see the world provides us with a richer and clearer understanding of reality. That understanding should enable us to pause and consider the humanity of others whose perceptions of reality are different from our own. In addition, that insight should make clear which of our would-be leaders will make decisions based on evidence, rational analysis, and an understanding of which solutions are likely to solve the problems we face. When we endeavor to understand and control the fictitious perceptions and outdated impulses of our genetic chaperones, we will be joining with others who seek to create a world that our Stone Age ancestors never imagined.

Epilogue

Two friends who critiqued the nearly completed manuscript asked me to explain what I understand reality to be in light of the strange reality of quantum mechanics. My explanation can be found on seeingrealityasitis.com under "Essays."

Appendix A

How is our emotional brain able to reason?

The pre-human brain, from which our brain evolved, was able to function emotionally but was not able to reason. For us to reason, Nature had to evolve our brain from what it was millions of years ago to what it is today. Brain parts of particular interest are shown in Figures 1 and 2 below. **In the process of acquiring the ability to reason, evolution grew existing parts and added new parts and capabilities as it adapted our brains to environmental challenges.**

The primitive brain began as a brain-stem that was one step above a rudimentary nervous system. It surrounded the top of the spinal cord and controlled basic body functions, such as breathing, metabolism, reflexes, and coordinated movement. It could react to stimuli such as the smells of prey, enemies, danger, sex partners, and the like. As it was evolving to become better at discerning water-borne and air-borne molecules, the smell-sensing part (olfactory bulb) was growing larger and beginning to encircle the top of the brain-stem.

Adapting the body to respond to things in the environment was becoming more complex and more specialized. The few neurons that orchestrated emotional responses gradually evolved into large almond-shaped structures (amygdalae) on either side of the brain-stem. Similarly, neurons that began to recognize and "remember" the factual information associated with smells and other sensory information evolved into the hippocampus (short-term memory). The combination of remembering factual details and their associated emotions enabled the amygdala and hippocampus in a crude way to recognize patterns in incoming sensory information and to produce a remembered response appropriate to the incoming pattern. The process was fast enough to initiate an attack or avoidance response in a few milliseconds (*milli-* is 1/1000).

Over time, sensory information flow was becoming complex and the few neurons that converted sensory information into a form usable in the brain evolved into the thalamus. Smell information, for example, was received by the thalamus, converted into a usable form, and sent to the amygdala and hippocampus. As this team of organized brain parts was evolving, the olfactory bulb was beginning to form around the brain-stem. The word "border" in Latin is *limbus,* and the bordered brain-stem became known as the "limbic system."

Additional neurons in the limbic system provided enhanced emotional capabilities that improved survival. In addition to rage and sex drive, the limbic system had enhanced learning and memory. Smells could be remembered, compared, and recognized, and emotional responses appropriate to the smell could be implemented. As the limbic system evolved, it became more broadly involved with communication throughout the brain. Our ancestors were beginning to perceive their environments, and what they perceived was a competitive and dangerous place with extreme survival challenges.

As brain evolution continued, the amygdala and hippocampus of the limbic brain, which are primarily responsible for our emotions, learning, and remembering, became capped by the neocortex—a large mass of folded neurons that, in part, processes reasoning. This occurred about 100 million years ago when mammals were becoming established. As the neocortex formed, neural pathways connecting it to the thalamus provided it with information necessary to enable the prefrontal lobes to analyze what should be done about incoming sensory information. **With this new arrangement, the thalamus now fed sensory information directly to both the amygdala and the neocortex. However, studies using rats show that information moves from the thalamus to the amygdala in about twelve milliseconds, while information from the thalamus to the neocortex and then to the amygdala takes about 24 milliseconds. This means that the amygdala can provide an emotional response to a situation before the reasoning neocortex can respond. In essence, the reasoning neocortex is not "wired" to prevent the implementation of a response from the emotional amygdala.** While this arrangement provides fast survival responses in life-threatening situations, the more circumstances evoke an emotional response; the less rational thought will prevail. For this reason, crimes of passion (committed in "hot blood") are punished less harshly than premeditated or rational crimes (committed in "cold blood"). The law recognizes that we need to consider how the human brain functions.

Medial view of right brain hemisphere

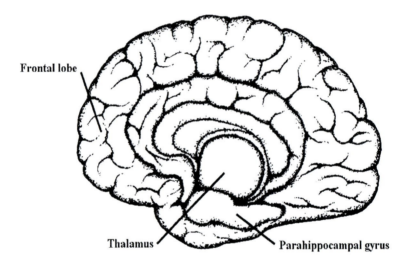

Figure 1

Specific limbic brain components

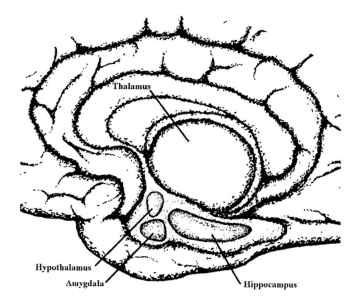

Figure 2

Appendix B

Propaganda and belief manipulation

Our belief inheritance is beset constantly by organizations, governments, mythologists, causes, and individuals who need our cooperation to achieve their goals. Public opinion is at the core of modern politics and commerce. In non-totalitarian governments, it is difficult, if not impossible, to survive politically against public opinion. Negative revelations about politicians or businesses can force them out of office or out of business. For this reason, people in influential positions "power surf" by staying ahead of the dominant beliefs of their power base, and polling public opinion provides the information they need to stay on the wave. In Franklin Roosevelt's time, the metaphor was to stay ahead of the parade, but not too far. People with power are seen to make decisions consistent with their own beliefs. If the public believes the "wrong" thing, public opinions can be changed by using propaganda or fake news to build a consensus. This requires that you convince people to believe in your goal. The operative word is *convince*, which derives from the Latin *vincere*, to conquer.

To convince is to conquer

The underlying principles involved in the process of influencing public opinion are not complex. Events are merely sensory data until they become perceptions in the mind. If belief alters perception, then how we perceive something depends on what we believe about what we observe. And if our beliefs can be biased through propaganda (priming, stereotyping, etc.) then propaganda influences our perception of events. This is why propaganda that undermines our belief about someone's motives, values, *et cetera*, destroys our ability to perceive that person's words or deeds correctly. For this reason, polls of public opinion are of questionable value. By polling what we believe today, a media strategist can contrive and deliver propaganda to influence tomorrow's polls. Otherwise stated, if today's polls reflect yesterday's propaganda, then of what value is a propagandist's claim that his or her position is supported by the polls? If polls reflect the effectiveness of someone's propaganda, then such polls are of little value in determining the unmanipulated opinion of the public. This problem is compounded by our tendency to believe what we prefer were true (motivated reasoning, dysrationalia, etc.).

President Bill Clinton was extremely good at managing his public image through his use of media management.[1] One example of his skill followed his refusal to provide the Food and Drug Administration with power to bar imports of substandard food. When a story appeared in the *New York Times* describing how federal inspections of imported food had plummeted

122

just as regulators were finding more outbreaks of food-borne diseases, President Clinton invited the press to the Rose Garden, where he proposed giving the FDA power to ban imports of substandard food. In addition, his press secretary even commended the New York Times for bringing the problem to light.[2]

The rise of secular mythology

Have you ever heard of Edward Bernays? *Life* magazine included him in a list of the one hundred most influential Americans of the 20th century.[3] Your encyclopedia probably describes him as a nephew of Sigmund Freud and the father of public relations. In talks with his uncle, when Freud described the workings of the non-conscious mind, Bernays saw an opportunity for the social elite to retain power by applying discoveries about the mind to control public opinion. The world was approaching the First World War and democracy was challenging control by the elite class, of which Bernays was a part. It became clear that to continue social and economic influence, elites had to covertly manage public perceptions to retain control.[4]

The human ability to reason is relatively new in our evolutionary history. It requires mental discipline and a willingness to change beliefs that reason shows are wrong. Until perhaps the past million or so years, our ancestors interacted with their surroundings, not with the aid of reason, but with non-conscious, intuitive, impulsive emotions and biases. Those primitive, unreasoning responses are so strong in our nature that reason plays a secondary part in the day-to-day thinking of many. Added to this is that our psychogenetic inheritance provides us with culture-specific stereotypical responses and emotions. When we act in concert, those stereotypical responses satisfy an inborn need we have to be part of a group. Knowing this and other aspects of our non-conscious nature, knowing which people and things we fear, envy or hate, propagandists manipulate our non-conscious mechanisms to control our beliefs and behaviors. What this means in a world filled with propaganda is that forming public opinion is more analogous to herding sheep than it is to well-reasoned debate.

In addition to Edward Bernays, John Hill, Carl Byoir, Ivy Lee, Elmo Roper, George Gallup, and others, a journalist named Walter Lippmann (1889–1974) became interested in propaganda. Early in the 20th century, Lippmann reasoned that democracy presupposes a rational electorate. This was an Enlightenment view held by the framers of the American Constitution. However, if most of us use primitive emotional mechanisms and symbolism instead of reason, Lippmann thought, the government cannot function unless a rational and responsible elite shapes public opinion to support governmental policies. His books, *Public Opinion* and *The Phantom Public*, contain his ideas on how such a democracy could be achieved. He believed that most of humanity perceived events not objectively but through mental images, which did not provide a correct view of reality. In addition, he thought that the average person's perception of reality became less accurate as the world became more complex, and as events were perceived less through personal experience and more through the mass distribution of the perceptions of others. It followed that the ability to control the access of news media to events was the key to managing public perceptions and opinions.

This is the reason public relations is such a clandestine business. If manipulation is to be effective, no one must know what the manipulators are doing. Lippmann determined that the public's stereotyped approximations of reality could be manipulated most easily through visual media, in part because images required less thought and were better able to elicit strong responses if the viewer related personally to the subject matter of the images.[5, 6] Lippmann used visual media to focus the public's emotions into symbols and to position selected public figures to embody those symbols in the mind of the public.[7, 8]

Edward Bernays thought that Lippmann's *Public Opinion* was too theoretical and abstract. **In** Bernays' book, *Propaganda*, he wrote that the group mind's first impulse is usually to follow the example of a trusted leader. Bernays was particularly interested in using the details of the human subconscious to his advantage. Today, securing the endorsement of trusted public figures to sell everything from coffee machines to government policy is so common that we do not consider when or why it began.

Bernays saw public relations experts as puppeteers who pulled the public's psychological strings to control chaotic public thinking to achieve the goals of the power elite.[9] He described propaganda as facilitating an "invisible government"[10] and the public relations counsel as those who induced the public to perceive reality in a preferred way.[11] In one example of this, a PR firm in Washington creates campaigns that appear spontaneous. They manufacture public displays by special interest groups and deluge Congress or the White House with faxes, letters, and phone calls that appear to reflect genuine public sentiment.[12] People in the public relations business know the organizing of these "grassroots" groups as "Astro Turf Organizing."[13] A Washington rally in support of a proposed "big government" health plan was reported to have been attended by people from the health insurance and health care industries posing as ordinary citizens.

Just as "grassroots" has its public relations "Astro Turf", science has a fictitious public relations version—junk science. The tobacco industry used junk science for decades to confuse the public regarding valid scientific research, which showed that smoking tobacco products was harmful. With the willingness of public relations firms to lie so convincingly to manipulate the public's emotions and perceptions, it should come as no surprise that major corporations with "image problems" were among the first clients of public relations firms. Stuart Schackne, vice-president of Standard Oil of New Jersey (SONJ), commented on a company public relations film at a 1948 Public Relations Conference. He described the film as an achievement in creating an emotional experience that connected the company with the public on a psychological level.[14] More recently, attempts by polluting corporations to improve their images without altering their polluting ways have involved something akin to whitewashing. They use the symbols and wording of environmentally responsible organizations, but the words and symbols are false. This is called "greenwashing." An example of greenwashing is changing the name or label of a product to invoke images of the natural environment, even though it contains harmful ingredients.

In another example, prior to the Gulf War with Iraq, a fifteen-year-old Kuwaiti girl reported that Iraqi soldiers in an occupied Kuwait City had removed Kuwaiti babies from their incubators and placed them on hospital floors to die. The story was widely circulated and repeated often. It clearly characterized the Iraqi military as barbarians and undoubtedly biased the American public against Iraq. The girl, a self-described hospital volunteer, had testified along with others before the Congressional Human Rights Caucus on October 10, 1990. It was stated at the hearing that the girl's identity would be kept secret to ensure her safety.

Inasmuch as news stories are seldom verified, the source of this story did not become general knowledge. Had this story been investigated, the following facts described in *PR!*[15] would have come to light. The girl was the daughter of the Kuwaiti Ambassador to the United States. That she witnessed any atrocities is dubious. The meeting of the Congressional Human Rights Caucus was arranged by Gary Hymel, a vice-president of Hill and Knowlton, a large public relations firm. Hymel also provided the other witnesses. The Kuwaiti royal family in exile retained Hill and Knowlton to manufacture American public support for military action against Iraq. The hospital atrocity story was part of a larger plan to demonize Iraq and to condition the public to support U.S. military intervention.[16]

If we are string puppets with propagandists working our genetic and psychogenetic strings, how shall we know what is true? Has a new era of secular mythology begun? Perhaps William James' vision of our reality is correct. He equated our beliefs to paper money in that they are deemed acceptable as long as they are not challenged.[17] By selecting or eliminating specific "facts" (beliefs), prolonged propaganda has reshaped cultures in much the same way that selective breeding has reshaped domesticated animals. Manipulation of history by politicians and clerics is an example of this image-improving process. It goes without saying that *properly practiced public relations does much to assist various interests in getting their story before the public.*

Belief management is known by many names—public relations, propaganda, positive and negative advertising, spin, disinformation, distortion, demonization, misrepresentation, half-truths, suppression (of opposing views voter participation, or truthful reports), censorship, one-sidedness, fabrication, exaggeration, minimization, and the like. Whatever it is called, it is all "belief management."

One means of influencing public opinion is to bias people very early in a debate. We find it difficult to suspend judgment and readily accept information to reach conclusions quickly. Unfortunately, early bias (apperception or priming) damages our ability to perceive subsequent information correctly. Bias influences belief, and belief alters perception. Similarly, a thing perceived when we are angry or afraid is likely to be perceived differently when we are tranquil. What we believe the future holds for us influences our perception as well. Is the glass half full, half empty, or too big? These influences on our perceptions are manipulated by propagandists to create self-serving beliefs. Their work is made easier when we want to believe the propaganda. Speech or images with strong emotional content are the stuff of which propaganda is made. **Speakers who invoke God, country, children, the needy, our fears, resentments, hatreds, and so on, or who demonize their opponents or others, are attempting to bias our thinking while avoiding discussion of the real issues. Speeches that make you feel instead of think are probably propaganda.**

An ideal campaigner for public office is a consummate convincer. An ideal office holder is ethical and able. We usually elect the convincer and hope that he or she is ethical and able. When we buy the package without knowing the contents we aren't making an informed decision. The common thread that runs through politics, journalism, and entertainment is that their most prominent people are the most believable. They are the best convincers, and given that they have the same abilities it's not surprising that they can move effortlessly from one such occupation to another. Some eyewitness accounts of Adolph Hitler's political rallies describe audiences as appearing mesmerized. Hitler began his speeches by speaking very softly. As he went on, his volume and demeanor would become more pronounced. By the time he finished speaking, he was often pounding on the lectern. It is conceivable that, in addition to using propaganda techniques, Hitler might have used a trance-inducing method to establish a receptive brain state in his audiences, perhaps similar to that used in the early 1700s during an evangelical and revitalization movement in America called The Great Awakening. In that movement, protestant ministers delivered passionate sermons that caused some parishioners to enter a trance-like state and to have a born-again experience.[18]

In addition to the news media, our information comes to us through the political process. However, the political process values gaining and holding power over everything and, to this end, dispenses misinformation (what was once called lies) about the attributes of its candidates and the deficiencies of their opponents. It is a battle for our beliefs, and to the extent that false information is believed, informed decisions are an illusion.

The complex interactions of evolving science, technologies, economic strength, social trends, propaganda, and myriad other factors determine which forces will most influence our psychogenetic evolution. Further complicating the quality of our information is that journalism is a commercial enterprise run by people with beliefs, emotions, and economic interests that influence their perceptions of reality. These biases are evident when the media turn a blind eye to the faults of people or organizations of which they approve, or when they refuse to allow publication of views that they oppose. In order to control market share, some journalists or news organizations find a crisis where there is none and sell it as news. When this happens, information is distorted and public understanding suffers.

The recent rise of citizen journalism, with unverified "news" being disseminated quickly over the internet, is a significant development, and its effect is now being analyzed. What we do know so far is that propagandists are using "citizen journalism" as a new tool. For example, it is likely that you have received propaganda on social media or in the form of an unnamed person's email that originated at a PR firm on K Street in Washington, DC, or at a secure building in Russia, eastern Europe or the like, that used a false quote by Thomas Jefferson or other ruse intended to instigate liberal vs. conservative animosity.

It seems that the news and entertainment businesses focus on the sensational roughly within a context of contemporary views of propriety. As they do, the belief-altered perceptions of events they create are like circus mirrors that distort while they reflect their audience's beliefs and values. It is a self-reinforcing process that gives prominence to the sensational and reinforces resultant changes in social views by representing previous aberrations as normal. Confirmatory bias being what it is, we will likely select media sources that reflect rather than challenge our view of the world.

Control of modern media has fallen into the hands of a few large corporations and wealthy individuals. Owning social media companies, television and radio stations, newspapers, and the like has made it possible for such special interests to manipulate public opinion. They are able to corrupt public perceptions of reality by providing self-serving interpretations of what information is presented, or by ignoring the social consequences of social media platforms that are willfully blind to the damage they do in pursuit of profit. With this power, the public can be led to believe that what is in the best interest of such entities is in the best interest of the public. Given the three branches of government—the executive, legislative, and judicial—only the judiciary is relatively insulated from the power of such special interests. An exception to this is when judges are elected or when their appointments are subject to elite influence.

In a recent attempt by the U.S. Senate to pass a law to resolve issues of damage to the public caused by the tobacco industry, a bill that came out of committee with an overwhelming vote (nineteen to one) was defeated in a Senate vote after an enormously expensive propaganda campaign orchestrated by the tobacco industry. Senators were intimidated into voting against the legislation by threats to prevent their re-election through distorted advertising directed against them individually. Through promises of favorable advertising, they were induced to vote against the legislation.

Failing a legislative resolution of how tobacco companies should be held liable for the damage they have done by using junk science to misrepresent the deleterious effects of the products they sell, a jury in Florida returned a verdict against the tobacco industry and awarded damages large enough to threaten the industry's future. In addition, State attorneys general banded together in a settlement negotiation with the tobacco industry to resolve outstanding litigation. State attorneys general were less influenced by tobacco industry propaganda and were freer to exercise the power of government to control an industry capable of manipulating public opinion through propaganda. However, since then, large corporations are reported to have begun making contributions to the political parties of attorneys general, which are associated with multi-day "golf outings" to which state attorneys general are invited in order to meet with representatives of major corporations.

Suppression of news about another piece of legislation, one which provided broadcasting high-definition television bandwidth to television companies *without charge*, was another coup of corporate media. Arguments against the giveaway *were not reported by the major news organizations*, in particular, those television news organizations owned by companies that stood to gain from the giveaway. With the public unaware of the giveaway, lobbying by media corporations was successful. Lest you think that controlling access to information is new, consider those who burned books or banned their reading, as with the burning of the Library of Alexandria in part by religious zealots, the destruction of libraries of indigenous peoples during European conquests in Central and South America, and the Roman Catholic Index Expurgatorius (banned book list.)

Today, through biased control of the media, or by misdirection using propaganda or irresponsible social media practices, power elites corrupt what the public believes and thereby what businesses, governments, religions, and other entities do. If we permit this to continue by interpreting the constitutional protection of free speech to extend to corporations and their army of propagandists, whose purpose is to thwart free speech, we are probably jeopardizing the right of future generations to open debate intended by the U.S. Constitution.

Not long after the fall of the Soviet Union, a highly educated Russian citizen in St. Petersburg, Russia, told me she was angry with the Communist party because she had been exposed to so much propaganda that she didn't know which of her beliefs were false. Since that conversation, I have thought about which of my valued beliefs might be old propaganda.

Unpleasant though it may be, propagandists are acquiring enormous amounts of our personal information and are becoming increasingly effective at manipulating our beliefs and behaviors. As they do, those of us who fail to understand and manage the vulnerabilities of our genetic chaperones will become the string puppets of political, religious, and business propagandists.

Appendix C

Self-organizing knowledge

Understanding the process by which our brains evolved can provide an insight into how our minds and beliefs came to be. Many of us believe that biological evolution is simply the result of competition between predators and prey, or of competition between or within species for the same resources, with the losers becoming extinct and the winners evolving. As it turns out, influences on the process of natural selection include the properties of biologically active matter, the solar system and Earth's characteristics, the sun, the moon, other planets, comets, asteroids, the Earth's axis tilt, climate change, continental drift, volcanoes, Earth's natural resources, circumstances that cause or disrupt genetic isolation, glaciation, the tendency of species to produce more offspring than the environment can support, ionizing radiation, and the possible gravitational effects of nearby stars. They have all played a role in shaping the evolution of life on Earth.

Self-organizing knowledge and Darwin's discovery

Of the countless ways in which molecules combine, some combinations are able to record,

reproduce, and adapt knowledge. Some organic molecules have "learned" to self-replicate by experiencing various arrangements that Nature selected based on trial and error. This process is analogous to Nature taking a multiple-choice test with no limit on the number of times it can take the test. After repeatedly submitting answers by guessing different choices, and after perhaps hundreds of millions of years, the blind trial and error selection of molecular arrangements eventually produced self-replicating "living" matter from non-living matter. The British philosopher Karl Popper (1902–94) saw biological evolution as a process of knowledge acquisition. He said, in essence, that the trial and error survival process of natural selection increases the genetic knowledge contained in the surviving DNA.[1]

DNA is the self-replicating organic molecule that records the knowledge needed to produce biological organisms such as ourselves. It is the material of our chromosomes and genes, and it determines our physical makeup and our inborn traits. DNA consists of two long chains of nucleotides (molecules) twisted into a double helix (twisted ladder) joined by hydrogen bonds and/or geometric compatibility[2] between the complementary nucleotides (base pairs) adenine and thymine or cytosine and guanine. It replicates when the double helix ladder of base pairs is unzipped along its length by an enzyme. Thereafter, each half of the helix selectively attracts from the immediate surroundings the correct missing nucleotides necessary to replace the unzipped nucleotide half. Self-organizing nucleotides thereby produce two complete DNA strands from an unzipped strand.

In Nature, DNA sequences of the fittest life-forms are replicated in their offspring, while DNA sequences of unfit life-forms go extinct when they die before reproducing. This trial and error process, by which knowledge self-organizes into successively better-adapted DNA sequences over generations, is what we see as biological evolution. There are two primary ways by which DNA sequences change: by externally caused mutation and by sexual reproduction. Mutation occurs when things like defective replication or exposure to ionizing radiation, carcinogenic chemicals, damaging viruses, or free radicals alter the nucleotide sequence. Of the two kinds of sexual reproduction, asexual or self-replicating reproduction causes a life-form, such as a bacterium, to replicate its DNA exactly. This produces offspring that are identical to the parent unless something causes its DNA to mutate. By comparison, sexual reproduction causes sections of DNA from each parent to combine. The resulting hybrid DNA produces an offspring that is different from both parents. By this process, sexual reproduction can create new generations with different DNA combinations.

Are there means other than DNA that cause knowledge to self-organize? By combining mathematics and electronics we have created computers capable of recording, reproducing, and adapting knowledge. A well-known way to accomplish a task with a computer is to write a series of instructions called code or a program. The code instructions are then executed by the computer to achieve some result. This type of programming relies on human logic and planning and, if some condition is not accounted for in the instructions, the program can malfunction or "crash" when the unexpected condition is encountered. With this type of programming, a computer does not acquire knowledge or adapt.

Can computer code be written such that, unlike traditional programming, it can adapt to circumstances and accumulate knowledge? In the early 1950s, John Henry Holland was researching this problem at the University of Michigan.[3] On reading evolutionary biologist R. A. Fisher's book, *The Genetic Theory of Natural Selection*, Holland realized that mathematical code, analogous in function to Nature's genetic code, could be developed to produce the equivalent of biologically evolved knowledge in a computer. The mathematical analog of DNA would be a genetic algorithm. Such an algorithm would comprise a recipe of instruction sets (genetic information) which, when executed by a computer processor, would cause actions relevant to the algorithmic organism. Such organisms would have no physical being, but would live and reproduce as organized bits of data in a world of information. They would have no intelligence except in the way they would function to optimize themselves to survive in a constantly changing informational environment. Holland developed a genetic algorithm that was a DNA-like computer-resident entity capable of acquiring knowledge from experience. With the ability to adapt to its environment entirely on its own, the genetic algorithm provided the remaining element needed for computers to achieve self-organizing knowledge.

Creating simple genetic-algorithm-based organisms was a start. **The question in Thomas Ray's mind was whether it was possible to create a genetic-algorithm-based ecosystem in a computer.**[4] Thomas Ray was teaching at the University of Delaware in 1989 when he began a most ambitious project. **He planned to create genetic-algorithm-based organisms that survived by competing for computer processor time and memory space in a computer memory environment he called "Tierra."** Processor time was needed to execute and reproduce their "genetic" code, and memory was the space in which they recorded and reproduced themselves. The actual process Ray created was more complicated than the following description of Tierra.

Tierran organisms entered a circular queue, and each in turn received a slice of processor time from the computer's central processor. The act of processing an organism's code copied it to another part of the memory environment and, on occasion, the replication resulted in a "child" organism in need of its own memory space and processing time. To enable Tierrans to evolve, alterations in their algorithm's genetic code were introduced in a number of ways. Some bits of their genetic code were changed at random, other bits were changed during replication, and still others during code execution. Death came to all Tierran organisms, but not at the same age. If their code adapted appropriately, they lived longer. Death was essential to keep Tierra from becoming overpopulated and thereby exhausting its supply of memory.

So much for theory. On January 3, 1990, after two months of programming, **Ray introduced the first Tierran into its carefully structured computer environment. The "creature" was 80 instructions long and was known as "Ancestor."** Contrary to the predictions of many, everything worked. Descendant clones were created and, in time, the oldest organisms began to die. Mutants appeared that were 79 instructions long and soon outnumbered the original Ancestor population. Soon, creatures with shorter instruction sets evolved a way to replicate as well. They had an evolutionary advantage because their reduced number of instructions enabled them to produce more offspring for a given number of central processor cycles. They were more efficient.

Then something new appeared in Tierra. A creature with 45 instructions began to compete for the position of most numerous creature. It would alternately outnumber the next most numerous creature and then its numbers would decline and soon rise again. What was happening? Creatures of fewer than about 60 instructions should not possess enough information to replicate. To replicate they had to be borrowing replication code from another creature. The new organisms had to be parasites. With fewer instructions needed to reproduce, their numbers increased rapidly. However, as their host organism's numbers declined, so too did the parasites. This accounted for the alternate surging of parasite and host populations. Mutating hosts soon evolved immunity to the parasites and virtually destroyed the parasite population as the new host population became dominant. However, mutating parasites evolved a way to defeat the immunity and the battle continued. **Without human intervention, Tierra was experiencing the same measure–countermeasure process so familiar in biological systems. Tierra was ten minutes old and knowledge was already self-organizing and adapting.**

Ray was able to do things with his artificial ecosystem that are virtually impossible with biological systems. He could analyze to the smallest genetic level what changed with each generation of Tierrans. In one experiment he turned off the mutation processes and found that mutations continued. His analysis suggested that parasitic tampering with host genetic code caused "sloppy replication." This suggests that parasites alone might account for some of the diversity we find in biological systems.

In experiments that ran for a very long time, long stable periods were followed by bursts of diversity— what is called "punctuated equilibrium" in biological systems. In one example, a single Ancestor evolved descendants and parasites. In turn, hosts evolved immunity. This relationship remained stable for millions of computer processor cycles. Suddenly, hyper-parasites appeared. They had the same number of instructions as the Ancestor, but almost one-fourth of the instruction sets (genome) was different. The now-dominant hyper-parasites eliminated parasites. A long period of stability followed. In time, hyper-parasites evolved a more efficient symbiotic method of reproduction. They began sharing code needed for replication. The new hyper-parasites could not reproduce without another hyper-parasite that could provide the reproductive code they needed. It was a kind of sexual reproduction. Although it was a more efficient way to reproduce, this change provided new parasites an opportunity to flourish. **The stable period ended as newly mutated hyper-hyper-parasites thrived on intercepted reproductive code as it passed between hyper-parasites. Tierra had evolved the equivalent of a venereal disease.**

Recent research shows that computer-simulated organisms can use increasingly complex defenses to evade parasites and thereby live longer than similar organisms with simpler genetic code. The research showed that host organisms that experienced frequent random mutations were better able to evolve defenses against infection. These "switching" mutations were nearly ten times more common in better-adapted host organisms.[5]

Work done by William Daniel Hillis at M.I.T.[6] with computer-based organisms indicated that, during long stable periods, mutations continue to accumulate at the genetic code level even though organisms show no outward appearance of change. When a threshold number of mutations result in an evolutionary advantage, those mutations spread rapidly through the population. Is it possible that the punctuated equilibrium we see in Earth's fossil record, such as during the early Cambrian period, resulted from the accumulation of unseen genetic mutations during periods of apparent stability?

Do the similarities of evolutionary processes in molecular and algorithmic knowledge systems establish that biological evolution is only one example of the concept that knowledge will self-assemble given sufficient time and appropriate means for recording, reproducing, and adapting information? **Does the concept of self-organizing knowledge suggest that the difference between randomness and order merely depends on whether interacting environmental constituents can accumulate knowledge and the amount of time random chance has operated?**

Our experience with self-organizing knowledge has led to a number of innovations. Self-adaptive robotic devices and artificial limbs are common. A new engineering discipline called "genetic programming" is solving design problems using self-adaptive computer programs. This system defines what needs to be done rather than how to do it.[7] Such programs can evolve the shape of a lens given only the focal requirements of light passing through it.

Even though we understand the process of genetic self-organization well enough to replicate organic evolution in inorganic environments, still some of us find it difficult to understand how such a process can evolve complex structures and organs such as eyes and wings. We know that feathers evolved from scales by accumulating genetic mutations that created successively longer scales, which gradually became more feather-like, perhaps to provide warmth in colder regions. Later, animals with such mutated scales were better able to escape predators as they leaped from trees because the feathers that evolved for warmth enabled them to glide farther than their shorter-scaled cousins. The enlarged pectoral fins of flying fish are a much simpler example of such an evolved adaptation. In their case, they escape predators by jumping into the air and flapping their pectoral fins to enable them to re-enter the water far from their pursuer. Flying fish with mutations that increased the size of their pectoral fins had an evolutionary advantage. In addition, species can evolve interdependently or coevolve as species adapt to each other's changes. It occurs between predators and prey and between insects and the flowers they pollinate.

Why are giraffes' necks so long? Some assume that their necks grew longer to enable them to eat from the tops of trees. Is that true? If the trees giraffes ate from gradually got taller, their necks might have grown longer in a process of coevolution. Otherwise, giraffes' long necks might appear to be inexplicable. Are we correct in assuming that acquiring food is the evolutionary motivation for their elongated necks? **Could they have evolved long necks for the same reason some birds evolved long tail feathers—as a mating advantage?** A giraffe's long, swinging neck and stubby horns make a formidable weapon, and we observe that male giraffes swing their necks in an attempt to horn-butt their rivals when competing for females.[8] More complex organs, such as eyes, involve a complex sequence of evolutionary adaptations. A detailed analysis of apparently incomprehensibly evolved body parts and organs is addressed in Richard Dawkins' books *Climbing Mount Improbable* and *River out of Eden.*

Much as past arguments against biological evolution cited the "inexplicability" of the giraffe's neck, contemporary critics of biological evolution use an argument called "irreducible complexity." This argument contends that taking away any part of a complex biological structure, such as that of a bacterial flagellum (a molecular motor with a rotating shaft that drives a screw-like propeller), will result in the failure of the design. In other words, because evolution works on the whole organism, it would have to bring together all of the elements of a bacterial flagellum *at the same time* for evolution to have produced that particular molecular arrangement. Planning, on the other hand, would do just that. And, inasmuch as planning requires intelligence, a god would explain the bacterial flagellum. While there are a number of logical evolutionary pathways that explain how the bacterial flagellum came together, supporters of irreducible complexity have not explained how their more complex planning god came together.

Genetic knowledge in the form of adapted body parts, such as differently shaped bird beaks, is what led Darwin to discover the mechanism of natural selection. His voyage on the *Beagle* laid before him a pattern of physical variations, including fossil remains, which Darwin recognized to be the result of natural selection. The Ancient Greeks were aware of natural selection, but could not explain why it happened beyond observing things like birth defects as a potential cause of extinction. Darwin's insight was that every part of reproducing a life-form is subject to variation (mutation) from generation to generation, and variations that better adapted a life-form to its changing environment were what Nature was selecting. It would be another century before molecular biologists would discover that it is DNA that stores genetic knowledge and that mutations in DNA molecules cause the variations that Darwin observed. Darwin also described genetically learned *behavioral* attributes. Such an attribute is what causes a frog to sit motionless as a snake passes within inches. In addition to smell (which is not highly directional), the snake's genetic knowledge resides in its sensitivity to motion. The frog's genetic knowledge resides in its inborn response to remain motionless.

Before we had the brain capacity to know that we had them, we relied on innate or instinctive behaviors such as sex drive, child rearing, tribal loyalty, or herd instinct. If you have not thought of inborn behaviors as genetic knowledge, then consider the behavioral responses of animals incapable of rational decision-making. Urges, emotions, biases, imprinting, and the like are genetic knowledge evolved by natural selection that enables animals to survive and reproduce. Although rational thought helps, only a few life-forms possess it. The rest manage quite well with their genetically evolved behaviors.

In the following quote from *On the Origin of Species by Way of Natural Selection,* Darwin described the accumulation of genetic knowledge in terms of inheritance (remembering), profitable variations (new knowledge), and non-survival (forgetting):

> How do those groups of species, which constitute what are called distinct genera, and which differ from each other more than do the species of the same genus, arise? All these results . . . follow inevitably from the struggle for life. Owing to this struggle for life, any variation, however slight and from whatever cause proceeding, if it be in any degree profitable to an individual of any species, in its infinitely complex relations to other organic beings and to external Nature, will tend to the preservation of that individual, and will generally be inherited by its offspring. The offspring, also, will thus have a better chance of surviving, for, of the many individuals of any species which are periodically born, but a small number can survive. I have called this principle, by which each slight variation, if useful, is preserved, by the term of Natural Selection, in order to mark its relation to man's power of selection [selective breeding]. We have seen that man by selection can certainly produce great results, and can adapt organic beings to his own uses, through the accumulation of slight

but useful variations, given to him by the hand of Nature. But Natural Selection, as we shall hereafter see, is a power incessantly ready for action, and is as immeasurably superior to man's feeble efforts, as the works of Nature are to those of Art.

The difference between selective breeding and natural selection is that in the former we choose which offspring survive, and in the latter Nature chooses.
Although Darwin was not aware of DNA, he could see the effects of DNA mutation, which he described as "any variation, however slight and from whatever cause proceeding." Today, we have mapped the DNA of many organisms and have built machines that can recreate DNA segments (nucleotide sequences) to an impressive degree. Given the knowledge contained in DNA maps or genomes, and an appropriate means for gestation, our technology should be able to reproduce extinct organisms.

Self-organizing psychogenetic knowledge

Is it possible that beliefs possess many of the properties of genes? Are proffered beliefs the genes of social evolution that cause cultures and other social organisms to evolve or to become extinct? **On the supposition that proffered "beliefs" influence cultural evolution as genes influence biological**

evolution, I refer to them as "psychogenes" (sI'kOH-jEEns) or mind-genes.

For a belief to survive over successive generations, it must experience a chain of transmissions to others who perceive the psychogene to have acquisition value. For this reason, fundamental or core psychogenes typically deal with matters having general relevance over many generations. Psychogenes cease to exist or become unused, for example, when they are perceived to be irrelevant, are superseded, or are no longer believed to be true. Simply stated, while Darwinian evolution is driven by natural selection, psychogenetic evolution is driven by the perceived value of a psychogene to the one who proffers it and to a potential recipient. It is necessary to use "perceived" as a condition because, for example, formative beliefs learned from a trusted source give those beliefs high acquisition value, even though the recipient might never have questioned the beliefs.

Alternatively, changing social conditions, exposure to foreign psychogenes, peer pressure, or simply misunderstanding the relevance or importance of a psychogene might result in it not being transmitted for lack of being proffered or for lack of perceived value to a potential recipient. Although, in the strictest Darwinian sense, beliefs can have survival value, clearly not all beliefs relate to survival. As they evolve, self-replicating heritable beliefs adapt to reflect the changing nature of the believers, their then-existing belief system, and things such as their physical and social environments. Core beliefs can be thought to define an organization, culture, or body of knowledge. A group's constitution, laws, or other rules are formal listings of their core beliefs.

The four DNA code letters A, T, C, and G, and the four RNA code letters A, U, C, and G are used by Nature to create the "words" used by biological evolution. In essence, the physical properties of carbon-based molecules have determined Nature's alphabet, but is it the only alphabet capable of recording information? With the evolution of human intelligence, another form of information recording came about in the form of belief systems. Our belief systems organize knowledge not as genetic sequences, but as systems of beliefs that define our cultures.

With the development of language, it was possible to collect, organize, discuss, and teach what had been learned. Our ancestors were able to organize their thoughts by manipulating words and concepts in their minds. Words enabled them to record important events and other information in the form of stories. With the development of increasingly complex language, psychogenetic evolution created more complex belief systems. In addition, a crucial genetic mutation, which appears to have evolved during the past 500,000 years, gave our ancestors the mental ability to ask why things are the way they are. In other words, instead of just perceiving their world with their five senses, humans are able to question the existence of unseen causes or intentions that produced what their senses perceived. Humans have the ability to perceive a chain of intentionality in others to about five levels. For example, I speculate that you think I believe that others plan to interfere with me based on their perception of my needs. This process is addressed by what is called the theory of mind. It is thought that brain mutations that made it possible to perceive intentions in this way evolved because they provided a group survival advantage.

When writing was invented, about 5,000 years ago, human social evolution accelerated. Complex thoughts could be recorded on clay tablets for later examination and study. By inventing language and writing, our ancestors created the first information age.

Although such things are difficult to date accurately, it is estimated that rudimentary language began to develop approximately 100,000 years ago. Writing began as pictographic markings on clay tablets in Sumeria about 5,500 years ago and in Egypt at about the same time. The oldest evidence of writing that represented the sound of speech (phonetic writing) is from Sumeria about 4,300 years ago.[9] With writing, we began to preserve and publish our beliefs. We had achieved with writing, and our ability to reason, what DNA had achieved with nucleic acids, and trial and error selection. Today, our libraries and other repositories of information contain the psychogenetic equivalent of our DNA.

It appears that all human social evolution prior to the development of writing, as important as it was, is minor compared with what has happened since. Compared with biological evolution, psychogenetic evolution has been explosive. While biological evolution is dependent on random mutations, psychogenetic evolution can take place using inductive and deductive reasoning. To paraphrase Mark Twain, it is like the difference between a lightning bug and lightning. By recording beliefs in the neural networks of our brains, by replicating them through psychogenetic transmission and by adapting them to changing circumstances by choosing which psychogenes we pass on and acquire, in my view, Nature has demonstrated another form of self-organizing and self-adapting knowledge. Whether that knowledge comprises organized ignorance or a clear understanding of reality is determined by the degree to which we see reality as it is.

Inasmuch as you have read this far, I assume that you are interested in knowing how to pronounce my last name. It is jo-von-no-lee. If you found the book interesting, please do me a favor and leave an honest review on Goodreads, Amazon, or perhaps recommend it to an appropriate academic department or your public library.

Notes

Chapter 1

If there is only one reality, why can't we agree on what it is?

1. Quoted from Dr. Donald Hoffman's 2015 TED Talk entitled "Do we see reality as it is?" To watch the full talk, visit TED.com.
2. Regarding nurture/Nature questions, please keep in mind that an individual's life experience biases are not the focus of this book.

Chapter 2

How biases and brain traits influence our perceptions

1. Quoteinvestigator.com, Henry Ford attribution.
2. Napolitano, Christopher M., and Veronika Job. "Assessing the implicit theories of willpower for strenuous mental activities scale: Multigroup, across gender, and cross-cultural measurement invariance and convergent and divergent validity." *Psychological Assessment*, 2018. DOI: 10.1037/pas0000557.

3. Von Hippel, William, and Robert Trivers. "The evolution and psychology of self-deception." *Behavioral and Brain Sciences* 34, no. 01 (2011): 1–16.

4. Westen, Drew, Pavel S. Blagov, Keith Harenski, Clint Kilts, and Stephan Hamann. "Neural bases of motivated reasoning: An fMRI study of emotional constraints on partisan political judgment in the 2004 US presidential election." *Journal of Cognitive Neuroscience* 18, no. 11 (2006): 1947–1958.

5. Emmons, Natalie A., and Deborah Kelemen. "The Development of Children's Prelife Reasoning: Evidence From Two Cultures." *Child Development*, 2014. DOI: 10.1111/cdev.12220. Boston University. "Belief in immortality hard-wired? Study examines development of children's 'prelife' reasoning." *ScienceDaily*, January 27, 2014. www.sciencedaily.com/releases/2014/01/140127164835.htm

6. University of Oxford (July 14, 2011.) "Humans 'predisposed' to believe in gods and the afterlife." *ScienceDaily*. Retrieved December 1, 2011, from http://www.sciencedaily.com/releases/2011/07/110714103828.htm

7. Lieberman, Matthew D., Johanna M. Jarcho, and Ajay B. Satpute. "Evidence-based and intuition-based self-knowledge: an FMRI study." *Journal of Personality and Social Psychology* 87, no. 4 (2004): 421.

8. Lieberman, Matthew D., Johanna M. Jarcho, and Ajay B. Satpute. "Evidence-based and intuition-based self-knowledge: an FMRI study." *Journal of*

Personality and Social Psychology 87, no. 4
(2004): 422.

9.   Lieberman, Matthew D., Johanna M. Jarcho, and
Ajay B. Satpute. "Evidence-based and intuition-
based self-knowledge: an FMRI study." *Journal of
Personality and Social Psychology* 87, no. 4
(2004): 422.

10. California Institute of Technology. "Pinpointing
the brain's arbitrator: Reliability weighed before
brain centers given control." ScienceDaily.Com
www.sciencedaily.com/releases/2014/02/14020513
3254.htm (accessed March 29, 2016.)

11. Jack, Anthony I., Jared P. Friedman, Richard E.
Boyatzis, and Scott N. Taylor. "Why do you
believe in God? Relationships between religious
belief, analytic thinking, mentalizing and moral
concern." PloS one 11, no. 3 (2016): e0149989.

12. Amodio, David M., John T. Jost, Sarah L., Master
and Cindy M. Yee. "Neurocognitive correlates of
liberalism and conservatism." Nature
Neuroscience 10, no. 10 (2007): 1246–1247.

13. Witteman, Cilia, John van den Bercken,
Laurence Claes, and Antonio Godoy. "Assessing
rational and intuitive thinking styles." *European
Journal of Psychological Assessment* 25, no. 1
(2009): 39–47.

14. Fugelsang, J. A. "Cognitive style and religiosity:
The role of conflict detection." *Memory and
Cognition* 42 (2014): 110.

15. Jack, Anthony I., Abigail J. Dawson, Katelyn L.
Begany, Regina L. Leckie, Kevin P. Barry, Angela
H. Ciccia, and Abraham Z. Snyder. "fMRI reveals
reciprocal inhibition between social and physical

cognitive domains." *NeuroImage* 66 (2013): 385–401.

16. Zhang, Li-fang. "Validating the theory of mental self-government in a non-academic setting." *Personality and Individual Differences* 38, no. 8 (2005): 1915–1925.
17. Johnson, Wendy, Eric Turkheimer, Irving I. Gottesman, and Thomas J. Bouchard. "Beyond heritability twin studies in behavioral research." *Current Directions in Psychological Science* 18, no. 4 (2009): 217–220.
18. Block, Jack, and Jeanne H. Block. "Nursery school personality and political orientation two decades later." *Journal of Research in Personality* 40, no. 5 (2006): 734–749.
19. Why do some people prefer predictability while others prefer to experience risk and change? Behavioral neuroscientists studied these preferences (thinking styles) in animals. Their experiments examined two brain regions in particular: the orbitofrontal cortex region (OFC), which is involved with decision making, and the basolateral amygdala region (BLA), which shares in decision making and is involved with conditioned responses. Their experiments assessed the ability of animals to deal with predictable and unpredictable conditions. When the animals experienced unpredictability, it was found that the level of a brain protein called gephyrin rose in the BLA region. Inasmuch as gephyrin has been associated in other research to a strong preference for order and certainty, it appears that increasing gephyrin biases us to avoid risk. This connection is supported by other

studies that show animals that have a non-functioning BLA seek certainty and avoid risk. It appears that increasing gephyrin decreases the influence of the BLA on decision making. If we are genetically predisposed to produce higher levels of gephyrin than average when faced with uncertainty, the risk aversion associated with elevated gephyrin might contribute to creating what we see as a conservative thinking style. Journal references:

Alexandra Stolyarova and Alicia Izquierdo. "Complementary contributions of basolateral amygdala and orbitofrontal cortex to value learning under uncertainty." *eLife*, 2017; 6 DOI: 10.7554/eLife.27483.

University of California – Los Angeles. "Changes in brain regions may explain why some prefer order and certainty." *ScienceDaily*. www.sciencedaily.com/releases/2017/07/17070709 5811.htm (accessed July 9, 2017.)

20. The above post is reprinted from materials provided by Northwestern University. The original item was written by Hilary Hurd Anyaso. Note: Content may be edited for style and length. Florian Hintz, Antje S. Meyer, and Falk Huettig. "Encouraging prediction during production facilitates subsequent comprehension: Evidence from interleaved object naming in sentence context and sentence reading." *The Quarterly Journal of Experimental Psychology*, 2016; 69 (6): 1056. DOI:10.1080/17470218.2015.1131309. Northwestern University. "Conservatives and liberals do think differently: Research shows different ways of solving everyday problems

linked to political ideology." *ScienceDaily*, March 15, 2016.
www.sciencedaily.com/releases/2016/03/16031512
0953.htm

21. Decety, Jean, Jason M. Cowell, Kang Lee, Randa Mahasneh, Susan Malcolm-Smith, Bilge Selcuk, and Xinyue Zhou. "The negative association between religiousness and children's altruism across the world." *Current Biology* 25, no. 22 (2015): 2951–2955.

22. Stanovich, Keith E. "Dysrationalia A New Specific Learning Disability." *Journal of Learning Disabilities* 26, no. 8 (1993): 501–515.

23. Goleman, Daniel. Emotional Intelligence. 1994. Bantam Books, New York, p. 5.

24. Perspect Psychol Sci. 2018 Nov; 13(6): 770–788. Published online 2018 Sep 19. DOI: 10.1177/1745691618774270
PMCID: PMC6238178
PMID: 30231213
Conspiracy Theories: Evolved Functions and Psychological Mechanisms
Jan-Willem van Prooijen1,2 and Mark van Vugt1,3

25. Gardner, Daniel. "The Science of Fear." 2009. Penguin Group (U.S.A.) Inc., 375 Hudson Street, New York, New York 10014, U.S.A, p. 103.

26. Hussak, Larisa J., and Andrei Cimpian. "An early-emerging explanatory heuristic promotes support for the status quo." *Journal of Personality and Social Psychology* 109, no. 5 (2015): 739.

27. Alford, John R., and John R. Hibbing. "The Origin of Politics: An Evolutionary Theory of Political

Behavior." Perspectives on Politics 2, no. 4 (2004): 707–723: 710.

28. Ebrahim, Zak. *The Terrorist's Son: A Story of Choice*. 2014. Simon and Schuster, NY, p. 79.

29. Premack, David, and Ann James Premack. "Infants attribute value to the goal-directed actions of self-propelled objects." *Journal of Cognitive Neuroscience* 9, no. 6 (1997): 848–856.

Chapter 3

How genetic chaperones influence belief formation and cultural evolution

1. Dawkins, Richard. *The Selfish Gene*. 1989. Oxford University Press, New York, p. 192.

2. "Psychogene" was coined in 2000 by the author in his book *The Biology of Belief*.

Chapter 4

The origin of belief systems

1. Duke University. "Society bloomed with gentler personalities, more feminine faces: Technology boom 50,000 years ago correlated with less testosterone." ScienceDaily. ScienceDaily, 1 August 2014.

www.sciencedaily.com/releases/2014/08/14080117
1114.htm
Robert L. Cieri, Steven E. Churchill, Robert G.
Franciscus, Jingzhi Tan, and Brian Hare,
"Craniofacial Feminization, Social Tolerance, and
the Origins of Behavioral Modernity," Current
Anthropology 55, no. 4 (August 2014): 419–443.
https://doi.org/10.1086/677209
Robert L. Cieri et al. 2014. Craniofacial
Feminization, Social Tolerance, and the Origins
of Behavioral Modernity. Current Anthropology,
vol. 55, no. 4, pp. 419–443; DOI: 10.1086/677209

2. Campbell, Joseph. *The Hero with a Thousand Faces*. 1968, p. 19.
3. *Encyclopedia of Psychology*. 1994, Vol. 2, Ch. 6, p. 505.
4. Shaw, George Bernard. *Treatise on Parents and Children*. 2004. Fairfield, Iowa, 1st World Library, p. 126.
5. "Letter to Bishop Mellitus Written by Pope Gregory" (601 CE), http://www/Source.com/history/docs/mellitus.html ,10/5/99.
6. Encyclopedia Britannica. 1960, Vol. 5, p. 643.
7. Damon Centola and Andrea Baronchelli. "The spontaneous emergence of conventions: An experimental study of cultural evolution." *PNAS*, February 2015, DOI: 10.1073/pnas.1418838112.

Chapter 5

Belief system evolution

1. *The Western Tradition Transcripts*, transcribed by Thomas Michael Kowalick, PBS Adult Learning Service, Alexandria, Va., 1989, p. 26.
2. Silberman, Neil Asher. "The World of Paul." *Archeology Magazine*, 49, (Nov/Dec, 1996): 30.
3. Cicero, De re Publica, ii, 19. quoted in Durant, Will, *The Story of Civilization*. 1944. Simon and Schuster, Vol. 3, Bk. 1, Ch. 5, Sec. 4, Par. 1.
4. *The Western Tradition Transcripts*, transcribed by Thomas Michael Kowalick, PBS Adult Learning Service, Alexandria, Va., 1989, p. 29.
5. Salvian, iv, 15; vii, passim; and excerpts in Heitland, W.E., Agricola, 423, Boissier, II, 410, 420, and Bury, Later Roman Empire, 307, quoted in Durant, Will, *The Story of Civilization*. 1950, Vol. 4, Bk. 1, Ch. 2, Sec. 3, Par. 4.
6. Whitmarsh, Tim, and Alfred A. Knopf. *Battling the Gods: Atheism in the Ancient World*. 2015. New York, English, 1st ed.
7. Frend, W.H.C. *Martyrdom and Persecution in the Early Church*. 2008. Cambridge: James Clarke & Co., 536–37.
8. Harari, Yuval Noah. *Sapiens: A Brief History of Humankind*. 2015. Harper Collins Publishers, New York, English, 1st ed., 215–16.
9. "Constantine The Great." Infopedia, Softkey Multimedia, Inc., Funk and Wagnalls' *New Encyclopedia* (CD ROM), 1996.
10. Tacitus, Histories; Annals, i.ll. TR Murphy, London, 1930, quoted in Durant, Will, *The Story of Civilization*. 1944, Vol. 3, Bk. 3, Ch. 13, Sec. 1, Par. 4.

11. Burckhardt, C.F., 252 F, quoted in Durant, Will, *The Story of Civilization*. 1944, Vol. 3, Bk. 5, Ch. 30, Sec. 3, Par. 1.
12. Hist. Aug., "Elagabalus," xxiv, 4, quoted in Durant, Will, *The Story of Civilization*. 1944, Vol. 3, Bk. 5, Ch. 30, Sec. 3, Par. 1.
13. Cf. Augustine, Ep. 232, quoted in Durant, Will, *The Story of Civilization*. 1950, Vol. 4, Bk. 1, Ch. 2, Sec. 3, Par. 5.
14. Machiavelli, "Discourses," iii, #1, quoted in Durant, Will, *The Story of Civilization*. 1957, Vol. 6, Bk. 1, Ch. 1, Sec. 4, Par. 10.
15. "Greece: John Paul begs forgiveness for Roman Catholics' history of sins against brothers." *The Los Angeles Times,* May 5, 2001.
16. McCabe, Joseph. *The Columbia Encyclopedia's Crimes Against The Truth*. 1950. Haldeman-Julius Publications, Girard, Kansas.
17. Kay, Aaron C., Jennifer A. Whitson, Danielle Gaucher, and Adam D. Galinsky. "Compensatory Control: Achieving Order Through the Mind, Our Institutions, and the Heavens." *Current Directions in Psychological Science* 18, no. 5 (2009): 264–268.

Chapter 6

Vulnerabilities of our belief systems and genetic chaperones

1. Kay, Aaron C., Jennifer A. Whitson, Danielle

Gaucher, and Adam D. Galinsky. "Compensatory Control: Achieving Order Through the Mind, Our Institutions, and the Heavens." *Current Directions in Psychological Science* 18, no. 5 (2009): 264–268.

2. University of Oxford. "Humans 'predisposed' to believe in gods and the afterlife." *ScienceDaily*, July 14, 2011. www.sciencedaily.com/releases/2011/07/1107141 03828.htm

3. Trigg, Roger, and Justin L. Barrett, eds. *The Roots of Religion: Exploring the Cognitive Science of Religion*. 2014. Ashgate Publishing, Ltd., UK.

4. Pyysiäinen, Ilkka and Marc Hauser. "The origins of religion: evolved adaptation or by-product?" *Trends in Cognitive Sciences* 14, no. 3 (2010): 104–109.

5. Turiano, Nicholas A., Benjamin P. Chapman, Stefan Agrigoroaei, Frank J. Infurna, and Margie Lachman. "Perceived control reduces mortality risk at low, not high, education levels." *Health Psychology* 33, no. 8 (2014): 883.

6. Ferguson, Michael A., Jared A. Nielsen, Jace B. King, Li Dai, Danielle M. Giangrasso, Rachel Holman, Julie R. Korenberg, and Jeffrey S. Anderson. "Reward, salience, and attentional networks are activated by religious experience in devout Mormons." *Social Neuroscience*, 2016; 1 DOI: 10.1080/17470919.2016.1257437.

7. Purzycki, Benjamin Grant, Coren Apicella, Quentin D. Atkinson, Emma Cohen, Rita Anne McNamara, Aiyana K. Willard, Dimitris Xygalatas, Ara Norenzayan, and Joseph Henrich. "Moralistic gods, supernatural punishment and

the expansion of human sociality." *Nature*, 530 (2016): 327–330.

8. Dunbar, R. (2005) *The Human Story: A New History of Mankind's Evolution*. London: Faber and Faber, p. 185.

9. Shenhav, Amitai, David G. Rand, and Joshua D. Greene. "Divine intuition: cognitive style influences belief in God." *Journal of Experimental Psychology*: General 141, no. 3 (2012): 423.

10. Dunbar, R. (2010) How Many Friends Does One Person Need? Harvard University Press. Cambridge, MA, p. 26.

11. Toner, Kaitlin, Mark R. Leary, Michael W. Asher, and Katrina P. Jongman-Sereno. "Feeling superior is a bipartisan issue extremity (not direction) of political views predicts perceived belief superiority." *Psychological Science* (2013): 0956797613494848.

12. Bastiaan T. Rutjens, Robbie M. Sutton, and Romy van der Lee. "Not All Skepticism Is Equal: Exploring the Ideological Antecedents of Science Acceptance and Rejection." *Personality and Social Psychology Bulletin* 2018, Vol. 44(3) 384–405 © 2017 by the Society for Personality and Social Psychology, Inc. Reprints and permissions: sagepub.com/journalsPermissions.nav DOI: 10.1177/0146167217741314 journals.sagepub.com/home/pspb

13. Hornsey, M. J., & Fielding, K. S. (2017). Attitude roots and Jiu Jitsu persuasion: Understanding and overcoming the motivated rejection of science. American Psychologist, 72(5), 459–473. http://dx.doi.org/10.1037/a0040437

14. Journal Reference:

Louis Martí, Francis Mollica, Steven Piantadosi, Celeste Kidd. Certainty Is Primarily Determined by Past Performance During Concept Learning. Open Mind, 2018; 1 DOI: 10.1162/opmi_a_00017

15. Cambridge Analytica a year on: 'a lesson in institutional failure', The Guardian, Sunday 17 March, 2019

Epilogue

No references.

Appendix A

How is our emotional brain able to reason?

No references for this appendix.

Appendix B

Propaganda and belief manipulation

1. Kurtz, Howard. *Spin Cycle*. 1998. Touchstone Books, New York, p. xiii.
2. Kurtz, Howard. *Spin Cycle*. 1998, p. xiii.
3. Ewen, Stuart. *PR! A Social History of Spin*. 1996. Basic Books, New York, p. 15.

4. Ewen, Stuart. *PR! A Social History of Spin*. 1996, p. 13.
5. Ewen, Stuart. *PR! A Social History of Spin*. 1996, p. 154.
6. Lippmann, Walter. *Public Opinion*, p. 234, quoted in Ewen, Stuart, *PR! A Social History of Spin*. 1996, p. 157, note 24.
7. Lippmann, Walter. *Public Opinion*, pp. 37–38, quoted in Ewen, Stuart, *PR! A Social History of Spin*. 1996, pp. 157–58, note 25.
8. Lippmann, Walter. *Public Opinion*, pp. 206–7, quoted in Ewen, Stuart, *PR! A Social History of Spin*. 1996, p. 158, note 26.
9. Bernays, Edward. *Propaganda*, pp. 27–34, quoted in Ewen, Stuart, *PR! A Social History of Spin*. 1996, p. 166, note 39.
10. Bernays, Edward. *Crystallizing Public Opinion*, p. 51, quoted in Ewen, Stuart, *PR! A Social History of Spin*. 1996, p. 167, note 41.
11. Bernays, Edward. *Propaganda*, p. 25, quoted in Ewen, Stuart, *PR! A Social History of Spin*. 1996, p. 167, note 43.
12. Engelberg, Stephen. "A New Breed of Hired Hands Cultivates Grass-Roots Anger." *New York Times*, May 17, 1993, pp. A1, A17, quoted in Ewen, Stuart, *PR! A Social History of Spin*. 1996, p. 29, note 5.
13. Ewen, Stuart. *PR! A Social History of Spin*. 1996, p. 29.
14. Schackne, Steward. "Some Considerations Underlying Jersey's Public Relations Activities." Standard Oil Company (New Jersey) and Affiliated Companies, 1948 Public Relations Conference, *Proceedings* (New York, October 21–

22, 1948), p. 82, quoted in Ewen, Stuart, *PR! A Social History of Spin*. 1996, pp. 384–5, note 15.

15. Ewen, Stuart. *PR! A Social History of Spin*. 1996, p. 28–9.
16. MacArthur, John R. *The Second Front: Censorship and Propaganda in the Gulf War*. 1992. New York: Hill and Wang, pp. 58–59, quoted in Ewen, Stuart, *PR! A Social History of Spin*. 1996, p. 29, note 4.
17. Ewen, Stuart. *PR! A Social History of Spin*. 1996, p. 40.
18. Edwards, Jonathan. *The Works of Jonathan Edwards*, Vol. 1, 1754, p. 112, Christian Classics Ethereal Library in PDF format.

Appendix C

Self-organizing knowledge

1. Popper, Karl. *Thought and Experience and Evolutionary Epistemology*. 1985. Quoted in Cristianini, Nello. *Evolution and Learning: An Epistemological Perspective*. March 21, 1995. University of Trieste, Italy.
2. "ATCG Puzzle Pieces." *Scientific American*. December, 1997, p. 22.
3. Levy, Steven. *Artificial Life*. 1992. Pantheon Books, New York, pp. 155–87.
4. Levy, Steven. *Artificial Life*. 1992, pp. 216–30.
5. Michigan State University. "Evolution: Complexity key propagating future generations." *ScienceDaily*. December 16, 2014.

www.sciencedaily.com/releases/2014/12/14121614
4139.htm

6. Kosa, David, Bennett, Forrest H., Keane, Martin
A., and Andre, John R., eds., *Genetic
Programming III: Darwinian Invention and
Problem Solving*. 1999. Morgan Kaufmann
Publishers, San Francisco.

7. Levy, Steven. *Artificial Life*. 1992, pp. 191–211.

8. Simmons, Robert. "How the Giraffe Got Its Neck."
Discovery Magazine. March 1997, p. 14.

9. James, Peter and Nick Thorpe. *Ancient
Inventions*. 1994. Ballantine Books, New York,
pp. 476–7.

Bibliography

Allegre, Claude J., and Schneider, Stephen H. "The Evolution of the Earth." *Scientific American* (October, 1994): 66–75.

"Anatomy of apprehension." *Science News* (November 9, 1996): 301.

"Anatomy of the Human Nervous System." *The Encyclopaedia Britannica,* Multimedia Disc. 1994–1998, Encyclopaedia Britannica Inc.

Armstrong, Karen. *A History of God.* New York: Alfred Knopf, 1994.

"ATCG Puzzle Pieces." *Scientific American* (December, 1997): 22.

Begley, Sharon. "Your Child's Brain." *Newsweek Magazine* (February 19, 1996): 55–62.

Bernays, Edward L. *Crystallizing Public Opinion.* 1923.

———. *Propaganda.* 1928.

"Biology isn't Destiny." *The Economist* (February 14, 1998): 83–4.

Bower, Bruce. "Brain cells work together to pay attention." *Science News* (March 11, 2000): 167.

———. "Bridging the Brain Gap." *Science News* (November 2, 1996): 280.

———. "Kids take mental aim at others' goals." *Science News* (September 18, 1995): 181.

———. "My Culture, My Self" *Science News* (October 14, 1997): 248.

———. "Rational Mind Designs." *Science News* (July 13, 1996): 24–8.

———. "The social brain: New clues from old skull." *Science News* (May 21, 1994): 326–7.

———. "Tots show signs of intentional minds." *Science News* (February 24, 1996): 118.

———. "Brain structure sounds off to fear, anger." *Science News* (January 18, 1997): 38.

Campbell, Joseph. *The Hero with a Thousand Faces.* Princeton: Princeton University Press, 1973.

Cavalli-Sforza, L.L., and Feldman, M.W. *Cultural Transmission and Evolution.* Princeton: Princeton University Press, 1981.

Connor, Steve. "God Spot is found in brain." *The Sunday Times (Britain),* November 2, 1997.

Corsini, Raymond J., Ed. *Encyclopedia of Psychology,* 2nd. New York: Wiley, 1994.

Cowen, Ron. "51 Pegasi: A star without a planet." *Science News* (March 1, 1997): 133.

———. "Bright Comet Poses Puzzles (Hyakutake's Tails of Mystery.)" *Science News* (June 1, 1996): 346–7.

———. "Chemical Pathway Links Stars, Meteorites." *Science News* (November 6, 1993): 292.

———. "New link between Earth and asteroids." *Science News* (November 6, 1993): 300.

———. "Opening the Door to the Early Cosmos." *Science News* (August 3, 1996): 68.

———. "The Once and Future Sun." *Science News* (March 26, 1994): 204–5.

———. "The real meaning of 50 billion galaxies." *Science News* (February 3, 1996): 77.

"Culture wars." *The Economist* (September 12, 1998): 97–9.

David, Kosa, Bennett, Forrest H., Keane, Martin A., and Andre, John R., Eds. *Genetic Programming III: Darwinian Invention and Problem Solving.* San Francisco: Morgan Kaufmann, Publishers, 1999.

Dawkins, Richard. *The Selfish Gene*, 2nd Edition. New York: Oxford University Press, 1989.

de Duve, Christian. "The Birth of Complex Cells." *Scientific American* (April, 1996): 50–57.

"Dioxin's fowl deed; Misshapen brains." *Science News* (August 30, 1997): 133.

Doyno, Victor. *Bible Teaching and Religious Practice, Mark Twain*. Reprinted in *Selected Writings of an American Skeptic*. Buffalo, New York: Prometheus Books, 1995.

"Dr. Gallop's Finger on America's Pulse." *The Economist* (September 27, 1997): 95–7.

Dukas, Helen, and Hoffman, Banesh, eds. *Albert Einstein—The Human Side*. Princeton: Princeton University Press, 1979.

Dunbar, Robin, *The Human Story*: London: Faber and Faber, 2005.

Durant, Will and Ariel. *The Story of Civilization*. New York: Simon and Schuster, 1935–1965.

"Earliest Earthlings." *Scientific American* (January, 1997): 29.

Ebrahim, Zak and Giles, Jeff (Contributor.) *The Terrorist's Son*, Simon & Schuster, New York, NY, 2014.

Engelberg, Stephen. "A New Breed of Hired Hands Cultivates Grass-Roots Anger." *New York Times*, May 17, 1993, A1, A17.

Erwin, Douglas H. "The Mother of Mass Extinctions." *Scientific American* (July 1996): 70–78.

Evans, Helen C., Wixom, William D., Editors, *The Glory of Byzantium, Art and Culture of the Middle Byzantine Era, A.D. 843-1261*, Metropolitan Museum of Art, N.Y, p. 84.

Ewen, Stuart. *PR! A Social History of Spin*. New York: Basic Books, 1996.

Fackelmann, Kathleen. "The Cortisol Connection." *Science News* (November 29, 1997): 350.

"Faith Steady Among Scientists—Or Is It?" *Free Inquiry* (Summer, 1997): 7–8.

Fitzgerald, Edward. *Rubáiyat of Omar Khayyám*. New York: Weathervane Books, 1985.

Frank, Adam. "In the Nursery of the Stars." *Discover Magazine* (February, 1996): 30.

Gehrels, Tom. "Collisions with Comets and Asteroids." *Scientific American* (March, 1996): 54–59.

"God, Science, and Delusion—a Chat with Arthur C. Clarke." *Free Inquiry* (Spring, 1999): 36–7.

Goleman, Daniel. *Emotional Intelligence*. New York: Bantam Books, 1994.

Hall, Manly P. *The Secret Teachings of All Ages*, 19th Edition. Los Angeles: The Philosophical Research Society, Inc., 1973.

"Hot Stuff." *The Economist* (August 24, 1996): 63.

"How brain cells make up their minds." *Science News* (October 28, 1995): 284.

Hume, David. *Enquiry concerning Human Understanding*. LaSalle, IL: Open Court Publishing, 1956.

Johnsen, Linda. "Evolution and Yoga." *Yoga International* (October/November, 1998): 35–9.

Kirshner, Robert P. "The Earth's Elements." *Scientific American* (October, 1994): 44, 59–65.

Kurtz, Howard. *Spin Cycle*. New York: Touchstone Books, 1998.

Levy, Steven. *Artificial Life*. New York: Pantheon Books, 1992.

Lipkin, R. "Early life: In the soup or on the rocks?" *Science News* (May 4, 1996): 278.

Lippmann, Walter. *Public Opinion*. New York: Macmillan, 1961.

MacArthur, John R. *The Second Front: Censorship and Propaganda in the Gulf War*. New York: Hill and Wang, 1992.

McCabe, Joseph. *The Columbia Encyclopedia's Crimes Against The Truth*. Girard, Kansas: Haldeman-Julius Publications, 1950.

"Memory building." *The Economist* (August 29, 1998): Electronic version.

Meslier, Jean. *Superstition in All Ages* or *Last Will and Testament*. New York: Truth Seeker Co., 1950.

"Mind Forming." *The Economist* (July 15, 1995): 63.

Monastersky, Richard. "The Moon's Tug Stretches Out the Day." *Science News* (July 6, 1996): 4.

———. "Impact Wars." *Science News* (March 5, 1994): 156–7.

———. "Jump-Start for the Vertebrates." *Science News* (February 3, 1996): 74–7.

———. "Popsicle Planet." *Science News* (August 29, 1998): 137–41.

———. "The first shark: To bite or not to bite?" *Science News* (February 17, 1996): 101.

———. "The Lost Tribe of the Mammals." *Science News* (December 14, 1996): 378–9.

———. "The pushy side of mammalian brains." *Science News* (November 18, 1995): 330.

———. "Walking away from a fish-eat-fish world." *Science News* (July 30, 1994): 70.

"A moon for Dionysus." *Science News* (September 27, 1997): 200.

Murphy, John Patrick Michael. "Hitler was <u>Not</u> an Atheist." *Free Inquiry* (Spring, 1999): 9.

Narayanaswami, K. (2011). Analysis of Nazi Propaganda. HIST S-1572: The Holocaust in history, literature, and film. Retrieved from http://blogs.law.harvard.edu/karthik/files/2011/04/HIST-1572-Analysis-of-Nazi-Propaganda-KNarayanaswami.pdf

"Neural development." *The Economist* (July 15, 1995): 62–3.

"Neural ties that bind perception." *Science News* (February 20, 1999): 122.

Nusslein-Volhard, Christianne. "Gradients That Organize Embryo Development." *Scientific American* (August, 1996): 54–55, 58–60.

"Old equipment finds big asteroid nearby." *Science News* (June 8, 1996): 365.

"Origin of Life on the Earth." *Scientific American* (October, 1994): 77–83.

"The Origin of Species." *The Economist* (November 25, 1995): 85–87.

Padian, Kevin, and Chiappe, Luis M. "The Origin of Birds and Their Flight." *Scientific American* (February, 1998): 38–47.

Peebles, P. James E., Schramm, David N., Turner, Edwin J., and Kron, Richard G. "The Evolution of the Universe." *Scientific American* (October, 1994): 53.

Pennisi, E. "Mice, Flies Share Memory Molecule." *Science News* (October 15, 1994): 244.

Popper, Karl. "Through the Experience of Evolutionary Epistemology." In Atti del convegno *Che cos'e il pensiero?* Accademia Nazionale dei Lincei, 1985.

Raloff, Janet. "Patients savor this brain disorder." *Science News* (June 7, 1997): 348.

———. "The Human Numbers Crunch." *Science News* (June 22, 1996): 396–7.

———. "When Science and Beliefs Collide." *Science News* (June 8, 1996): 360–4.

"Rational Mind Designs." *Science News* (July 13, 1996): 24.

Ramachandran, V.S. M.D., Ph.D., Sandra Blakeslee. *Phantoms in the Brain*, William Morrow Paperbacks (August 18, 1999)

Regalado, Antonio. "The Troubled Hunt for the Ultimate Cell." *Technology Review* (July–August, 1998): 34–41.

"Repeating DNA surprises once again." *Science News* (March 16, 1996): 171.

Ryan, William, and Pitman, Walter. *Noah's Flood*. New York: Simon & Schuster, 1998.

"Satellites hint sun is growing stronger." *Science News* (September 27, 1997): 197.

Schopenhauer, Arthur. *The World as Will and Idea,* 9th ed. New York: Scribner's, 1948.

Seppa, N. "Nailing Down Pheromones in Humans." *Science News* (March 14, 1998): 164.

Shaw, George Bernard. *Back to Methuselah: A Metabiological Pentateuch*. New York: Brentano's, 1929.

Shaw, George Bernard. *Treatise on Parents and Children*. Fairfield, Iowa, 1st World Library, 2004

Silberman, Neil Asher. "The World of Paul." *Archeology Magazine* (Nov/Dec, 1996): 30.

Simmons, Robert. "How the Giraffe Got Its Neck." *Discovery Magazine* (March, 1997): 14.

"The Slime Alternative." *Discover Magazine* (September, 1998): 86–93.

Stenger, Victor J. "Quantum Spirituality." *Free Inquiry* (Winter, 1997): 57–9.

Tornay, Steven C. *Ockham: Studies and Sketches.* La Salle, IL Open Court Publishing, 1938.

Travis, John. "How many genes does a bacterium need?" *Science News* (September 28, 1996): 198.

———. "Let's repeat: Mutation gums up brain cells." *Science News* (December 20/27, 1997): 390.

———. "Repeating DNA linked to schizophrenia." *Science News* (December 8, 1997): 294.

———. "The Ghost of Geoffroy Saint-Hilaire." *Science News* (September 30, 1995): 216–8.

———. "Third Branch of Life Bares Its Genes." *Science News* (August 24, 1996): 116.

———. "Yeast genetic blueprint publicly unveiled." in *Science News* (May 4, 1996): 278–8.

"Wake up, sleepy brain." *Science News* (September 21, 1996): 184.

Trigg, Roger, and Justin L. Barrett, eds. "The Roots of Religion: Exploring the Cognitive Science of Religion," Ashgate Publishing, Ltd., 2014.

Weinberg, Steven. "Life in the Universe." *Scientific American* (October, 1994): 59.

West, Thomas G. *In the Mind's Eye.* Buffalo: Prometheus Books, 1991.

"When glaciers covered the entire Earth." *Science News* (March 29, 1997): 196.

Winters, Jeffrey. "The Answer in the Voids." *Discover Magazine* (March, 1996): 27.

Zimmer, Carl. "Breathe Before You Bite." *Discover Magazine* (March, 1996): 34.

Acknowledgments

I want to express gratitude to my editor, LJ Markowitz, for her numerous editing suggestions that helped shape the final draft. Special thanks to Dr. Thomas Tonon for his excellent edits and suggestions regarding applying concepts developed in the book to current social developments. Thanks also to Shirley Wescott, Dr. Claudio Bruno, Joseph R. Giovannoli, and John Mickowski for their constructive comments and for finding time to critique my manuscript. I would also like to thank Thomas Giovannoli for his fine illustrations and The Expert Editor at experteditor.com.au for their first-rate service. The cover was designed by Giaccone & Smith Storytellers, Shelton, CT.

Pre-release readers

Gay Hartigan, Alexander McKenzie, Bernard Bober, Drew Giovannoli

Permissions acknowledgments

I gratefully acknowledgment the following for permission to reprint previously published material:

TED Talks excerpt from the talk by Dr. Donald Hoffman's 2015 "Do we see reality as it is?" To watch the full talk, visit TED.com.

Tim Tyler, on-memetics.blogspot.com for his listing of words and phrases used to describe units of culture.

The Philosophical Research Society, Inc.: Excerpts from *An Encyclopedic Outline of Masonic, Hermetic, Qabbalistic and Rosicrucian Symbolical Philosophy* by Manly P. Hall. Copyright © 1962 by The Philosophical Research Society, Inc.

Haldeman—Julius Publications: Excerpts from *The Columbia Encyclopedia's Crimes Against The Truth* by Joseph McCabe.

In addition to the above, grateful acknowledgment is made to authors whose copyrights have expired and to those whose quoted material falls within the category of fair comment.

Glossary

apperception

A perception process that causes us to interpret new experiences by transforming our perceptions to fit the narrative of our existing beliefs. This brain trait gives disproportionate importance to our childhood beliefs as they influence our perceptions later in life.

arbitrator brain region

The "arbitrator" brain region influences decision making by inhibiting the intuitive memory system when the arbitrator determines that reflective memory is more likely to produce a desired outcome.

biases

Genetic preferences and predispositions that disproportionately influence our perceptions of situations. Examples are the negativity bias and eternal existence biases.

bias blindness (for purposes of this book)

Being blind to biases and other aspects of our genetic chaperones is essential because being aware of its illusory perceptions would cause the illusion to be lost and render our genetic chaperones ineffective.

brain traits (for purposes of this book)

These are anatomical structures, neurological circuitry, and neurochemicals that influence our perceptions and thinking.

bubble reality

In groups, an unrealistic or improbable attribution of value or other characteristic(s) to people or things in social media, commercial, metaphysical, political, and other groups. The Salem witch trials and more recent conspiracy theories spread on social media are examples.

cognitive hacking

Cognitive hacking is a process that seeks to manipulate the perceptions of people by exploiting their psychological vulnerabilities. Recent examples are seen in social media fake news intended to alter elections around the world.

DNA

DNA refers to deoxyribonucleic acid. It comprises pairings of the organic bases adenine (A), guanine (G), cytosine (C), and thymine (T) in a long, twisted ladder-like molecule. Varying base sequences of AGC and T are referred to as the genetic code that determines the structure and other characteristics of living things.

dysrationalia

An inability to think and behave rationally, and to have difficulty in forming beliefs, and assessing belief consistency even with adequate intelligence. An example is the high percentage of members of Mensa in Canada that believe in astrology and that extraterrestrials have visited the Earth.

fake reality

When propagandists create artificial conditions calculated to trigger our Stone Age genetic chaperones, they cause us to think that the "fake reality" they create is real. Politicians, businesses, religions, individuals, and various organizations employ propagandists to achieve their goals by using our ego, fear, and the like to trigger responses that make fake realities believable.

genetic chaperone

Over generations of competing to survive, our ancestors' brains accumulated various genetic adaptations that improved their fitness to survive at the expense of their ability to see reality as it is. Those adaptations include mental biases, brain traits, and neurochemicals that influence our perceptions and behaviors by causing us to perceive a survival-enhancing version of reality instead of perceiving reality as it is. Collectively, our mental biases, brain traits, and neurochemicals are referred to as our "genetic chaperone."

genetic chaperone triggers

Propagandists use our psychological profiles to trigger genetic chaperone responses. In doing so, they manipulate our behaviors and beliefs. This was used on a grand scale in Nazi Germany.

neurochemicals

These are substances such as neurotransmitters and neuro-active drugs that influence brain activity. Mushrooms containing psilocin, for example, disrupt a part of our forebrain where thought, reasoning, and memory are processed. The disruption causes us to perceive artificial experiences (hallucinations).

neurotransmitters

These are substances such as norepinephrine, serotonin, dopamine, and endorphins that influence neurological systems. An example would be norepinephrine, which is involved in arousal, learning, and mood regulation.

organized ignorance

When our belief systems accumulate beliefs that have no basis in reality, they are organizing ignorance. This happens when our beliefs are based on reality-distorting perceptions such as magical thinking, dreams, hallucinations, illusory correlations, or the reality-distorting biases and traits of our genetic chaperones.

planning assumption

When we observe what appears to be the result of someone's intentional act, we assume that it was planned by someone or something, even if it just happened. This assumption is based on the intentionality bias, which apparently kept our Stone Age ancestors alive by causing them to default to perceiving threats. Today, the intentionality bias can have very different results. For example, Isaac Newton thought that the laws of Nature were intentional in that they revealed the same intentionality a watchmaker has in making a watch. In this case, his maker of the universe was God.

psychogene

A "psychogene" is a proffered belief. Psychogene is used instead of "belief" because it connotes both a belief component (psycho) and a (gene-like) component, which indicates that belief transmission is analogous to gene replication. While beliefs can have survival value, not all beliefs relate to survival. However, beliefs can evolve by adapting to the believer's changing circumstances. Psychogenetic transmission occurs when a belief becomes known (proffered) to someone who perceives it to have acquisition value, and transmission takes place (when the proffered belief is acquired or accepted). In addition, the phrase "psychogenetic evolution" is used to describe the gene-like process by which belief systems adapt to changing conditions.

psychogenetic transmission

Transmission of a belief from person to person (psychogenetic transmission) takes place when the belief is proffered (made known) to a potential recipient who perceives it to have worth to them (acquisition value), and who completes the transmission when the proffered belief is accepted.

reciprocal thinking regions

This refers to a brain arrangement of two separate but coordinated thinking regions. One region processes analytical thinking, and the other processes intuitive thinking. While these thinking regions are separate, they coordinate such that when one region is activated, the other is deactivated in a reciprocal inhibition relationship. One consequence of this arrangement is that when fear causes us to begin thinking in the intuitive thinking region, we will not be able to access the reason-based analytical thinking region to evaluate the situation.

theory of mind

The theory of mind includes the ability to attribute to others' perceptions and views that are different from our own. Such attributions can include the intentions, desires, perspectives, emotions, beliefs, and knowledge of others. Although we take that ability for granted, we acquired it within the past 500,000 years, and it is involved in our ability to ask why things are the way they are.

intentionality bias

This bias, among other things, causes us to perceive intent in the actions of others, even when there is none. We demonstrate this bias when we are about one year of age.

intuitive and reflective memory

Intuitive memory "averages" many experiences to form generalizations about our experiences. It is slow to form and slow to change. When an observation causes your intuitive memory to respond, you will not recall specific experiences that contributed to the intuitive memory, but you will experience a feeling, intuition, impression, suspicion, hunch, or insight about the new observation. Our other way of remembering is reflective memory, which can form and change with just one experience.

robotized followers

These are members of extreme groupthink groups who are conditioned using psychological manipulation to not think for themselves, to follow orders, to not ask questions, and to mindlessly endorse group beliefs. In addition to repetitious group rituals, the focusing illusion is used to create the perception that their beliefs are more important than they are.

self-organizing knowledge

Knowledge self-organizes if given appropriate means for recording, reproducing, and adapting information by way of trial and error selection. It is how our DNA drives genetic evolution and appears to apply to psychogenetic knowledge as well, where remembering, transmitting, and evolving beliefs are the basis of cultural evolution.

thinking styles

Of the numerous thinking styles we are born with, the two primary styles are conservative and liberal, which are not the same as political views. Examples of thinking style differences would be that risk-taking is associated with a liberal thinking style, while predictability is associated with a conservative thinking style.

two thinking-style advantage

Human groups have an advantage when they consider the perspectives and solutions of both liberal and conservative thinking styles. By combining thinking styles, they have a larger selection of perceptions and solutions to understand and solve problems. Winners-take-all groups, by giving excessive influence to either conservative or liberal thinking style members, limit the group's options and perspectives to those of the dominant thinking style.

Index

A

abortion clinic, 37
acquisition value, 42-45, 56, 58, 148, 183-84, 189
adaptation, *See also* evolution, 16-18, 143-44, 181
advertising, 43, 105, 128, 132
agreeableness mutation, 49
Alexandrian Library, 133
algorithm, 13, 17-18, 138-42
altered perceptions, 61, 100, 131
amygdalae, 53, 115-17, 156-57
  emotions and, 120
ancestor (computer program), 139-141
analogue computer, 82
animism, 51, 55, 83, 98, 108
  in ancestral beliefs, 55-56
  and modern religion, 50-51

anti-enlightenment, 98-99
artificial intelligence, 13, 106-07
apperception, 29-30, 44, 55, 93, 97, 98, 128, 179
  vagrant asking for money example, 29
Aquinas, Thomas, 88
Arab, 86
arbitrator of intuitive/reflective memory conflicts, 24-25, 179
asteroids, 135
astrology, 30-31, 181
Astro Turf organizing. 126
Augustine, a philosopher, 81, 84-85, 87-88, 93
Averroes, Moorish philosopher, 78, 81, 85
Axial Age, 66

B

bacterial flagellum, 144
bandwagon effect, 103-04

basolateral amygdala, 156-57

behavior/behavioral attributes, 17, 27, 35, 43-43, 53, 61, 73, 92, 100-01, 103-06, 124, 134, 145-46, 181-82

belief alters perception, 122, 128 *See also* apperception, beliefs, *See also* faith,

  psychogenes, 43, 45, 64, 66-67, 70-71, 76-78, 81, 148-50

  Ancient Greek, 50, 66, 68, 83, 95, 97, 145

  core, cultural, 46-50, 66, 83, 95, 97, 145

  early Christian, 70, 83

   irreversible, 45, 55

   perceived value, 148

   survival value of, 148, 183

   transmission, 43-45,150, 183-84

   transmission through children, 44, 55-57

Bernays, Edward on belief management, 39, 123-25

  work used in Nazi Germany, 39

belief manipulation, *See also* belief management,128

belief superiority bias, 96

belief systems, 13, 42, 44-45, 47, 55-56, 58-59, 61, 63-65, 69, 71, 76, 81, 89, 93, 95, 97-98, 108, 110, 148-49, 182, 184

  and organized ignorance, 55, 60-61, 151, 182

  persistence of, 55, 182

believer, true, 37

biases,

  focusing illusion, 22, 38, 97, 102, 186

  confirmatory, 21, 29, 85, 131

  illusion of control, 21

  illusion of superiority, 21, 96, 103-04

  motivated reasoning, 22, 122

  negativity, 21-22, 96, 103, 179

  optimism, 21

  self-serving, 21, 103-04

Gregory I, Pope, 57
groupthink,
    and extreme beliefs,
36, 38
    and the focusing
        illusion, 38
    and mind-guards,
36
    and robotized
        followers, 37, 39,
186
guanine sequences,
136, 180
See also DNA

H

hacking, cognitive,
106, 180
hallucinations
    achieved by and in
        dreams, 49, 52, 54,
182-83
Henry III, 86
Hill and Knowlton
 public relations firm,
127
Hillis, William Daniel,
142
hippocampus, role of
 in memory, 116-17
Hitler, Adolph, 39,
129
Hoffer, Eric, 37

Hoffman, Donald, 17-
18
Holland, John Henry,
138

I

ignorance, organized,
55, 60-61, 98, 151
illusion of control
 bias, 21
illusion of superiority
 bias, 21
illusory correlation,
20, 44, 54, 90, 92, 97,
183
information age, first,
150
inheritance,
    psychogenetic, 67,
124
Inquisition (of
 Medieval
 Christianity), 38, 86,
93
insight, *See* intuition,
24, 111, 135, 145, 185
intentionality bias,
32-33, 88, 91, 183, 185
internet, 39, 43, 59-
60, 104, 106, 130
internet and cyber-
    bubble reality, 60,
180

intuition, 24, 34, 51, 99, 185
Iraq, 127
irreducible complexity argument, 144
Islam, 87, 85
Italian evolution,
  beliefs, early, 64-65
  Christian (early), 70-83
  Empire phase of, 68
  Greco–Roman psychogenes and, 67, 70, 76, 81
  Greek psychogene assimilation, 67
  Oriental/Middle Eastern psychogenetic influence on, 70
  Renaissance, 81-82, 85, 87

J

John Paul II, Pope, 82

K

Kirkus, 12
Knowledge, *See also* organized ignorance, 13, 17, 44-45, 56-57, 80, 97, 127, 135-39, 140, 142-43, 145-50

self-organizing, 135, 138, 142
Kuwait, 127

L

Leibniz, Gottfried, 87
liberal thinking style, 26-28, 66, 88, 92, 95, 97, 186
Life magazine, 123
limbic system, 31, 116
Lippmann, Walter, 124-25
logical fallacies, 38, 101-03
Luther, Martin, 78, 81, 86

M

Machiavelli, Niccolò, 78-79
magical thought, origins of, 54
Marsilius of Padua philosopher, 81
matter, self-replicating, 136
Maxentius, Emperor of Rome, 75
McCabe, Joseph, 79-80
media, modern

communications, 38-39, 43, 58, 99-100, 105-07, 125, 130-31
memes, 41-43
memory,
reflective, 23-26, 92,179, 185
reflexive (intuitive), 23-28, 92-93, 123, 155, 179, 184-85
Mensa, 30, 181
metaphysical, bubble reality, 60, 180
Michelangelo Buonarroti, 50, 79
mind-genes, 148
See psychogenes
molecules.
self-organizing nucleotides, 136
moon, 49, 110, 135
Moors, 81
motivated reasoning bias, 22, 122
Milvian Bridge, battle of, 75
multiculturalism, 98
mutation, role in evolution, 11, 33, 49, 137, 141-43, 145, 147, 149-50
mystery, role of in mythology, 51
mysticism and ancestral beliefs, 53

mythology, 51, 53, 66-67, 72-73, 76, 88, 123, 128
eternal existence biases, 22, 74, 82, 90, 92
dreams and, 48, 51-52, 54, 92, 183

N

natural selection,
See also evolution, 33, 84, 135-36, 138, 145-48
Nazi, 38, 103-04, 182
negativity bias, 21-22, 96, 103, 179
neocortex in human brain, 31, 117
Neo-Platonism, 76, 83-84
neurochemicals, 18, 89, 180-82
neurons (cells), role in brain evolution, 11, 115-17
neurotransmitters, 28, 182
dopamine, 182
noradrenaline, 28
Newton, Isaac, 1873

O